REVOLUTIONARY PEDAGOGY

I0105804

Second Edition

REVOLUTIONARY PEDAGOGY

Primer for Teachers of Black Children

Molefi Kete Asante, PhD

Universal Write Publications LLC

New York, NY

REVOLUTIONARY PEDAGOGY PRIMER FOR TEACHERS OF BLACK CHILDREN

SECOND EDITION Copyright © 2023 Universal Write Publications, LLC

Library of Congress Control Number: 2023920755

ISBN: 978-1-942774-92-1

Printed in the United States of America.

Mailing/Submissions:

Universal Write Publications, LLC
421 8th Avenue, Suite 86
New York, NY 10116

Website: UWPBooks.com

This book has been partially supported with a financial grant from SAGE Publishing.

Contents

Dedication

Jamar Ramses, Ayaana, Aion, Nova, Akila and Akira
Who will always know and teach!

Acknowledgments

I acknowledge my immediate great ancestors, whom I knew, and their ancestors, whom I channeled for life itself. They are the victors because they saw strong men and women still coming long after they had tired of the fight against oppression and mental incarceration. I also recognize the sacred ground of the ancestors of the Native Peoples of this land and ask for forgiveness for trampling over the dust of their dead in ignorance. May my work show light to all of us.

I wish to acknowledge the enormous support given to me by my publisher, Ayo Sekai, whose infinite belief in the type of work I do has inspired me to continue to write every day. Over the years, I have published with many companies, but when I first presented my ideas to Ayo Sekai, I did not have to convince her of the importance of African agency as a concept. She immediately saw that the dislocation of Africans from the continent of Africa, and from traditions, customs, rituals, values, and philosophies, had a profound impact on behavior, knowledge, and relationships, making it necessary to advance a philosophy of Afrocentricity. To Ayo, I am very grateful.

In many ways, Ayo reminds me of SAGE Publications' founder, Sara Miller McCune, who heard the proposal for the *Journal of Black Studies* when I was 28 years old and accepted to become its publisher, thus making SAGE an inspiration and leader in African American scholarship as well as a model for the brilliance and entrepreneurial spirit of Ayo Sekai.

A host of colleagues in education have been exceptional thinkers, readers, and compatriots who I must thank for their support; therefore, to Joyce E. King, Susan Goodwin, Patricia Reid Merritt, Adam Urbanski, Aaron Smith, and Nah Dove, I give praise for being strong sounding boards for ideas. I acknowledge the invaluable suggestions from my exceptionally gifted son, M. K. Asante, who never missed an opportunity to give me good advice about his generation for much of what I know about contemporary culture, and to him I am truly obligated. I thank my daughter Eka, who writes to me, in the fashion of a past age, every day, so that I know I am not without her love and she, not without mine.

Finally, to Ana Yenenga, my wife, who endured with grace, some concern, and much more love than I deserve my inconvenient writing hours and my occasional zoned and focused moments when nothing mattered more than getting a sentence right, I lay at her feet, *me daa ase*, agreeing to take a break some time.

Preface

After the first edition of *Revolutionary Pedagogy*, I received an amazing response from teachers and educational professionals to the book. Their overwhelming reaction was that I had written a book that was helpful to those who wanted to have both a theoretical and a practical manual for pedagogy, especially in places where students of African descent were being taught. Of course, the fundamental principles included in this book are not limited to one ethnic community or one region; they are meant to aid teachers who have the courage to provide effective instruction to students.

At the very beginning of our now centuries-old sojourn in North America, Africans recognized in traumatic fashion the difference between our own institutions that had been put in place for thousands of years on the continent of Africa and the new ground of enslavement and brutalization that would be implemented by Europeans to teach subservience. Out of this awareness has come generation after generation of resistance to the brainwashing and mental programming of our people. We knew we were not who they said we were, and our ancestors, with whatever material and mental resources they had, fought to demonstrate the incredible originality of our children in learning, playing, and participating. No handicap was so great that it could not be overcome by a steady will to achieve.

It is not alarmist to say that education, as a system, has not always been our friend; indeed, the statistics of the condition of African American education suggest that education has systematically robbed Black children of their motivation, creativity, cultural identity, and assertiveness. This means that children often leave school more damaged psychologically and culturally than they could or would have been had they remained at home.

My concern as an educator and a consultant for the infusion of Afrocentric content into curricula has been how to teach teachers ways to unlock the potential in the children sitting directly in front of them in the classroom. I have tremendous faith in the possibilities of victories because I have never seen a student who *could* not learn. I have seen students who it is said do not learn. I have seen students who do not score well on standardized examinations. But I also know that I have never found a student I could not reach using pedagogy based in Afrocentric theory. What is truly remarkable is the degree to which this pedagogy can be taught and learned by thousands of teachers.

Today, the principal concern in public education is a commitment to excellence in all students. If a teacher learns the mechanisms of revolutionary pedagogy, all else falls into place. But as teachers, we must dedicate ourselves to the task of energizing our students to be and do their best, as a way to ensure their future and ours. So this book is written for teachers and teacher educators to stop the betrayal of urban children and the scapegoating of revolutionary teachers.

I have seen teachers criticized and not rewarded for their success in the classroom. These are the teachers who can reach children but who are often seen as "too ethnically committed" or "culturally sensitive" to their students or as believing in teaching "Black history every day." These are the teachers who principals and superintendents ought to see as outliers for the kind of pedagogy this book represents.

It is my deeply felt conviction based on my studies and experiences that teachers who utilize this revolutionary pedagogy will be among the most successful at teaching in urban centers. However, these principles are not merely useful for teachers of Black children; they are useful for the teaching of any children. A teacher must know something about the culture of the student to be considered an excellent teacher. Once you know your students or demonstrate an interest in knowing them by reading and inquiring, you will discover your own victories in the classroom. This is the theme of this book. I have addressed this book to those who have ears to hear and eyes to see the necessity of reversing the brain freeze that often accompanies not just students but also teachers who are placed in urban situations and have limited knowledge about how to proceed.

Molefi Kete Asante
Department of Africology
Temple University
Philadelphia, Pennsylvania

Notes on the Second Edition

After the COVID-19 crisis had reached its peak and was on the way down in the number of cases, several cities across the country seemed to experience a rise in the number of murders in their urban core. Young Black men, for example, in Philadelphia, Pennsylvania, where I live, were killing each other at a very rapid rate in 2022. As the head of a Black Studies program at a very large public university for nearly 30 years, I was often asked to comment on the reason for this outbreak of violence in the African American community. This question was put to me by journalists, community center directors, and ordinary citizens. My answer was always different from that of traditional activists, police, and social workers, who saw the issue from the perspective of their own disciplines and sought to find a solution by having more community centers, where the youth of the city could find other outlets for pent-up energies and emotions. Some thought that young people needed to be supervised by law enforcement and therefore neighborhoods needed more surveillance by the police. Still others felt that counseling sessions where parents and guardians or teachers were included might work the miracle. I could not disparage any of these answers or attempts at finding a solution because the problem was complex, beginning with the inability of our society to control young people's access to weapons. Guns in the hands of youth, just like guns in the hands of irrational adults, make for tragic and deadly results.

The answer for me was in education, a particular kind based on history and culture. Children who are taught their own history, which locates them within their own cultural space, have far more to present to the world than children who are left to drift on the social seas without sails. My own transformation from a peasant child in southern Georgia, with the lingering attitudes of an enslaved African population, to a university professor was through a profoundly valuable cultural education that I did not first get in kindergarten or elementary school but in high school in Mr. Merl Tharpe's African American history class. Reflection on this experience has provided me with a road map for a revolutionary pedagogy practiced by Mr. Tharpe without a name for it.

Entering the classroom with his right hand already pointing at one of us seated before the teacher of the 11th-grade class arrived, he would ask, "Young woman, who are you?" Meekly, the student would mention her name. Looking at the rest of the class with astonishment, Mr. Tharpe would ask, "Did I ask her to give me her name?" Thus began the journey of our mental liberation from the captivity of our bodies to the domination of our wills against the embarrassing appendages of the European names of the slaveowners. When the semester ended, we knew who we were, and we had a mission to teach others who they are. I have spent decades trying to fulfill Tharpe's directives, and that is why I am now able to see clearly the provocative reasons for a revolutionary pedagogy. Once students are introduced to it by teachers, they can take on their own obligation to teach others.

Molefi Kete Asante
Department of Africology
Temple University
Philadelphia, Pennsylvania
May 2023

CHAPTER 1
A Revolutionary Pedagogy

There is a general opinion among educators, politicians, and the public that urban education is a failure in the United States. Using the various indices of the new educational regime, researchers have found that schools in larger urban communities demonstrate lower scores on standardized tests, lower levels of discipline, more school absences, and often less motivation to learn. In its Executive Summary of School Conditions, the National Center for Education Statistics (NCES, n.d.) states,

> Many Americans believe that urban schools are failing to educate the students they serve. Even among people who think that schools are doing a good job overall are those who believe that in certain schools, conditions are abysmal. Their perception, fed by numerous reports and observations, is that urban students achieve less in school, attain less education, and encounter less success in the labor market later in life.

The NCES studied the situation and found that "forty percent of urban students attended these high poverty schools (defined as schools with more than 40 percent of students receiving free or reduced priced lunch." The NCES concludes that poverty alone cannot explain all of the differences between schools when one compares one set of high-poverty schools with another. In addition to poverty, one must examine issues of single-parent families, school mobility, television-watching time, absenteeism, pregnancy, and lack of high expectations. In my judgment, most of these factors are directly related to poverty itself, whether in rural schools or urban schools, but a substantial amount of responsibility lies with teachers.

All children can learn in normal settings. Gloria Ladson-Billings, one of the most astute theorists of education, understands this more than most, and that is why she has declared that few schools recognize what students themselves bring to the classroom. Taught for the most part with a pedagogy designed to maximize white cultural styles and objectives, Black children and Latino/a children, who constitute majorities in many large American cities, are often victimized by the pedagogy and the curriculum. In 2016, Ladson-Billings coauthored with William Tate the book *Toward a Critical Race Theory of Education*, which was an advance in our understanding of whiteness as a property, intersectionality, microaggressions, and counternarratives.

There are many scapegoats offered on the altar of explanation for the poor quality of urban schools. Some teachers and school administrators have blamed Black boys for some of the dysfunction found in urban schools. These evaluators tend to believe that if we can somehow fix the inner-city schools of large cities like Pittsburgh, Philadelphia, Atlanta, Houston, Detroit, Chicago, New York, Los Angeles, and St. Louis, we will be on our way to relieving American society of a negative aspect of education. The National Education Association (2011) concludes,

> The statistics describing Black boys as more likely than their peers to be placed in special education classes, labeled mentally retarded, suspended from school, or drop out altogether is disturbing enough. But the surprising news, at once puzzling and promising, is that we have tools to reverse this trajectory and success stories to prove it.

Thus, the National Education Association sees the statistics as disturbing but the prospects for success as promising. Any thesis about education that places the burden on children may be shouting at obvious outliers about what is wrong with the system. Black children are not responsible for the broken urban educational system; they are often victims of it. In her monumental book *The Afrocentric School*, Nah Dove (2021), the eminent educator, writes, "The institution of 'Education' has been absolutely vital to providing misinformation to enable people to know their 'roles' in society" (p. 9).

It is the educational system in the United States that is a failure, not urban schools, not Black boys, not teachers, but the overall system that denies children a proper education. Taking this or that sector out of the system and holding it under a microscope will not reveal the deeply flawed architecture of student and teacher disinterest in piecemeal fixes. Failure is not necessary; it must be designed, organized, and maintained to effectively mis-educate and misdirect the children the system is supposed to help succeed. The information and knowledge that will aid children in deciphering the society and making life better for themselves and those around them should not be foreign but should be familiar to them.

Immediately after the Nat Turner Rebellion in Southampton, Virginia, in 1831, the Virginia House of Delegates held several meetings to address the fear and insecurity that whites were feeling throughout the state. One delegate, Henry Berry, himself a slaveholder from the western part of the state, spoke on behalf of the gradual elimination of slavery. It was clear to him that nothing that whites could do would completely ensure their safety since the "Southampton affair" as they called it had shown that uneducated and illiterate Africans could rise up against them at any time. However, Berry (1831/1859) pointed out,

> Sir, we have, as far as possible closed every avenue by which light might enter their mind; we have only to go one step further—to extinguish the capacity to see the light, and our work would be completed; they would then be reduced to the level of the beasts of the field, and we should be safe; and I am not certain that we would not do it, if we could find out the necessary process and that under the plea of necessity. But, sir, this is impossible; and can man be in the midst of freemen, and not know what freedom is? (Redpath, 1859, p. 102)

Think of it, the light of knowledge had been denied to Africans already for just over 210 years, and yet Nat Turner, and others before him, rose up to glimpse the flash of the future liberation of Black people with a shining glory of optimism. Regardless of how much the enslavers sought to deny Africans the light and to reduce us to the "level of the beasts of the field," our ancestors kept alive the possibility of truth breaking through to the masses.

The enslavement (1619–1865), of course, was a period of utter fog, and even the little clarity that entered their minds was enough to convince our ancestors that they should have the same rights and privileges as those who held our people in bondage. What could have compelled whites to devise such a system but an attempt to stifle all intelligence and freedom? Numerous writers have quoted Berry out of context because they believed he was advocating a continuation of this practice, but in effect, he was despairing that the White slaveholders had done all they could to prevent Africans from recognizing their right to freedom and their dastardly acts had failed. He was amazed at the resilience, intelligence, and courage of the enslaved Africans who kept their eyes on freedom.

Of course, after the Civil War, the condition of Africans during the Reconstruction and into the 20th century was one of great desperation for education. Hundreds of whites from the northern states traveled to the South to assist Blacks in reading and writing and mathematics (Anderson, 1988). The activities were important, but in the end, they had to be seen as another way to undermine the historical and intellectual narrative of Africans. The education was to deepen in many cases, not to relieve the burden of ignorance about self.

I agree with the conclusion reached by Dove (2021), who argued that linking children to their cultural home is one way to awaken the desire for knowledge. If you break that link or never admit to it, you can prevent the growth of children's passion for learning; that is why respecting the link challenges perpetual falsehood.

Education, the genuine transmission of knowledge, is at the heart of transformation. I have always believed that the route to freedom leads through the *endarkening* avenues of historical and contemporary information. Self-knowledge for the African American is the first order of business in the classroom. Carter G. Woodson (1933/2013) discussed this in his famous book *The Mis-education of the Negro*. He made a powerful point in the Preface:

> It may be of no importance to the race to be able to boast today of many times as many "educated" members as it had in 1865. If they are of the wrong kind the increase in numbers will be a disadvantage rather than an advantage. The only question which concerns us here is whether these

"educated" persons are actually equipped to face the ordeal before them or unconsciously contribute to their own undoing by perpetuating the regime of the oppressor. (p. 3)

Woodson worried, as I have worried after years of working in education, that those who are the most educated, most qualified, and most promoted in their offices as teachers and administrators may not all understand the dangers that lurk in the academies educating children with the same principles and ideas of Eurocentric cultural norms present since the beginning of education in the United States. One of the reasons why African American scholars have always looked to Woodson as a nascent Afrocentrist is that he understood the power of comprehensive oppression. This is precisely why he wrote,

> No systematic effort toward change has been possible, for, taught the same economics, history, philosophy, literature and religion which have established the present code of morals, the Negro's mind has been brought under the control of his oppressor. The problem of holding the Negro down, therefore, is easily solved. When you control a man's thinking you do not have to worry about his actions. You do not have to tell him not to stand here or go yonder. He will find his "proper place" and will stay in it. You do not need to send him to the back door. He will go without being told. In fact, if there is no back door, he will cut one for his special benefit. His education makes it necessary. (p. 4)

The problem as Woodson (1933/2013) saw it was with the "educated" African American.

> The "educated Negroes" have the attitude of contempt toward their own people because in their own as well as in their mixed schools Negroes are taught to admire the Hebrew, the Greek, the Latin and the Teuton and to despise the African. Of the hundreds of Negro high schools recently examined by an expert in the United States Bureau of Education only eighteen offer a course taking up the history of the Negro, and in most of the Negro colleges and universities where the Negro is thought of, the race is studied only as a problem or dismissed as of little consequence. For example, an officer of a Negro university, thinking that an additional course on the Negro should be given there, called upon a Negro Doctor of

Philosophy of the faculty to offer such work. He promptly informed the officer that he knew nothing about the Negro. He did not go to school to waste his time that way. He went to be educated in a system which dismisses the Negro as a nonentity. (p. 5)

Perhaps the most iconic and most frequently quoted statement that Woodson (1933/2013) made was when he wrote,

If you teach the Negro that he has accomplished as much good as any other race he will aspire to equality and justice without regard to race. Such an effort would upset the program of the oppressor in Africa and America. Play up before the Negro, then, his crimes and shortcomings. Let him learn to admire the Hebrew, the Greek, the Latin and the Teuton. Lead the Negro to detest the man of African blood—to hate himself. (p. 88)

Woodson (1933/2013) was obviously relying on what he knew and experienced in the 1930s and earlier, but he was also prescient in understanding that the teaching of African Americans was the single most important activity to transform the lives of the oppressed. The term "Afrocentricity" did not exist when Woodson wrote his book, but one could today apply it to his strong thinking that Eurocentric education had not only disoriented African people but had also failed to educate Africans to appreciate their own contributions to civilizations. In some ways, the dissemination of the Eurocentricity of culture as an oppressive and universal mandate of white racial domination smashed the growth and emergence of African cultural maturity. It is this oppressive educational framework that is still playing devilish tricks on African American students.

In their brilliant book *The Afrocentric Praxis of Teaching for Freedom*, Joyce E. King and Ellen E. Swartz (2015) connect culture to learning in a demonstrative display of both good research and good common sense about how to approach education in general and the problem of failure in particular. Culture and learning are deeply intertwined in the process of socializing young people to understand their reality. They are not necessarily joined in the administration of school-based programs; administrators tend to like what they see as bringing hardware solutions to software problems. They encourage rote memory of unnecessary information if it is necessary to raise the scores of their children, thus enabling them to keep their jobs. This is puerile and venal thinking in my judgment and serves no other purpose than to find a scapegoat for the failure of the educational philosophy that leans too heavily on testing and not enough on making good citizens.

King and Swartz (2015) contend that the importance of heritage and cultural knowledge in education is fundamental, stating, "Heritage knowledge refers to group memory, a repository or heritable legacy that makes a feeling of belonging to one's people possible" (p. 29; Clarke, 1994). Boaventura de Sousa Santos's (2007) abyssal thinking proponents would dismiss this profoundly important aspect of the educational process. What King and Swartz have done is to make a connection between practice and theory in the teaching of children. Of course, I favor these theorists because I think that King and Swartz are two of the most important philosophers of education, but they are also practitioners in the best sense of teaching teachers. In some real ways, I gained a lot for my work in revolutionary pedagogy from their idea of *teaching for freedom*. This is about breaking out, escaping, and leaping toward freedom; one is truly a revolutionary teacher when one can show students how to break out for freedom.

I remember being in a classroom where a young girl, Maria, was chastised by her teacher because a group of us who were visiting had come into the room but the little fifth-grade girl had continued doodling on a piece of paper. The teacher called out to Maria to pay attention, but she continued to doodle. I walked over to the child's desk and looked at her drawings; they were fantastic, and I asked her if I might take a closer look at them. When she consented, I held the paper up and said to the group of visitors, the teacher, and the class, "These are truly beautiful drawings!" Everyone seemed quite pleased with the fact that she had been recognized. Maria beamed.

Of course, anyone who reads this book will also see that I have learned a lot from the leading antiracist intellectual in Canada, George Sefa Dei, whose book *Teaching Africa: Towards a Transgressive Pedagogy* (2010) remains one of the outliers for all progressive scholars. Dei argued that history is itself a discipline that introduced and maintained colonialism.

To overcome the tremendous hold that Eurocentric history has on African scholarship, it will be necessary to introduce what he calls a transgressive pedagogy. Obviously, one can see that I upped the ante and went for a more provocative term; however, it was not just the term "revolutionary" that I went for but also the idea that we needed a pedagogy that would overturn the stereotypical notions of African people wherever we were in the world. Furthermore, I saw that what happens to us as Africans happens to Native Americans, Arabs, Jews, Mexicans, and other people in other societies. A revolutionary pedagogy shows itself as an ethical thrust into the midst of racial, cultural, economic, psychological, and sectarian education.

Isolating components of the system and holding them up to criticism is a good exercise for exposure, but it is not enough to bring about revolution in any category. To change the situation, we will have to confront the philosophical approach to the process of transmitting information. Essentially, we need a revolutionary pedagogy.

Honestly, a revolutionary pedagogue needs to understand the ground on which she or he is standing. You must identify your own cultural referents since they will be at the beginning of all your thoughts about education. I have seen some self-hating people who blame their own self-loathing on others. If you do not know your culture or the culture of your students, you are bound to mess up in the classroom. I once had a supervisor who might be called a self-loathing Black person who tried to find everything negative she could about Black people, but she admired white culture to no end. It was her white underlings who eventually isolated her and brought her down from the position she held.

A revolutionary pedagogy will require different ways of thinking and maybe even different structural components of the school setting. I remember the book written by Shawn A. Ginwright a few years ago called *Black in School: Afrocentric Reform, Urban Youth, and the Promise of Hip-Hop Culture* (2004). What Ginwright recognized was the fact that we could not just keep doing the same old things and expect the results to be different. If we were bold enough to look at the way children and adults learn and then implement the kind of apparatus that would capture that learning style and interest, we would be looking behind the educational veil. I call this type of radical examination and suggestion a resetting of the school agenda that will liberate the teachers and students in a school building. While this is only one step in the right direction, it remains only one step because learning styles and teaching styles operate under the regime of a symbol and cultural system that dictates what and how children will learn. Let's revolutionize the system now!

Here is what I see in a revolutionary pedagogy where everything that has to do with the school is pedagogy. I see an emphasis on the five aspects of revolutionary pedagogy, *ethics*, *values*, *literacy*, *relationships*, and *reasoning*, as essential to upsetting the status quo. The first comment I will hear when I say these things is that this is what schools are already doing. Of course, this is not true because we would not have racists, homophobes, narcissists, and jerks coming out of schools with declared diplomas that they have been educated. In fact, what we call "good" schools are often some of the ones where we find the least educated people. They become the hotbeds of negative thoughts about diversity, multiculturalism, progressive projects to save the planet, Black Lives Matter protests, and fairness to Native Americans, on whose land we all live. To put it mildly, we have a system in need of a revolution, not one that has seen a revolutionary pedagogy. Dove (2021) believes that it is essential for this revolution to begin with Afrocentric schools and teachers who actually "get it" to make a difference. She writes,

> Depending on circumstances, not all educators involved in these schools may be highly literate, but their knowledge will be used and translated for children gaining literacy. What is of greatest importance is, as follows:
>
> • The *knowledge* of the teachers, children, and their local communities
> • The teachers' love for the children
> • The teachers' vision of a better world. (p. 10)

Dove (2021), with multiple cultural inputs from West Africa and the United Kingdom, created *The Afrocentric School* out of her UNICEF-supported research on African education. Dove trained interviewers to assist her in the nearly one-year examination of the methods used by Ghanaians outside the metropolitan centers of Accra and Kumasi in the education of children. Taking the principal values that undergird African families and highlighting them for her readers, Dove demonstrates that one must know where one stands culturally and psychologically to be able to learn correctly. *The Afrocentric School* advances this idea as part of a revolutionary pedagogy. I believe that the subtitle of the book, *BluePrint*, speaks to the need to provide a guideline as a foundational curriculum for children and teachers. Like any revolutionary intervention, *The Afrocentric School* provides an agency-centered perspective that allows the study of cultures, concepts, or historical narratives from the standpoint of the African child's heritage. The objective we have for education can influence pedagogy; that is why Dove's objective is to create students with character and good critical judgment.

If the aim of education is to teach students how to make money, then you will have to practice a pedagogy that will create the conditions for students to learn how to make money. Such a pedagogy may emphasize the big, beautiful, and rich business schools with famous names.

If the aim of education is to teach students how to worship and serve a divinity, then you will have a pedagogy that will encourage students to revere that which they neither know nor understand. Such a pedagogy may emphasize piety over curiosity, and subservience over creativity.

My point is that how one sees the purpose of education will dictate pedagogy. John Dewey (1903), the legendary American educator, says "that the general purpose of school is to transfer knowledge and prepare young people to participate in America's democratic society" (p. 194). Of course, this definition is woefully limited and limiting and speaks to the nativist orientation of much of American thinking in the early 20th century. However, the purpose of education for the revolutionary pedagogist is to prepare students to live in an interconnected global world with personal dignity and respect for all other people as human beings with the same privileges that one seeks for oneself, while preserving the earth for those who will come afterward. This is a revolutionary point of view that incorporates the five aspects of revolutionary pedagogy.

THE FIVE ASPECTS OF
REVOLUTIONARY PEDAGOGY

1. *Relationships.* We are all bound by the same human kinship. Any attempt to separate humans based on physical characteristics, religious beliefs, artistic attributes, or regional origins is anti-intellectual, anti-educational, and anti-human. The core of our humanity is our relatedness first to our family and then to our communities and other entities, political, religious, or artistic; but ultimately, we are bound together by our humanity.

2. *Ethics.* Ethics is a consciousness of the moral principles that work within the context of society and assists in the determination of what is harmful and what is useful for the community, nation, and world. Thus, all traits that support harmony, balance, order, truth, righteousness, justice, and reciprocity are at the core of the protection of humanity, the universe, and the self. Effective education introduces ethical ideals and provides students with a model for their own lives based on the survival of the human species.

3. *Values.* The idea of values suggests that there are standards that have the capacity to elicit an emotional response to persons, places, themes, and other phenomena. When a person does what is beneficial to society, we are inclined to say that the person has good values. One does not normally speak of bad values; indeed, values imply something that is good. In an interconnected world, for example, the sustaining of the world depends on recognizing global diversity and responding to global sharing with other human beings.

4. *Literacy.* Literacy is the state of being knowledgeable about a particular category of knowledge. For example, in the case of English, the person who can understand the language and express it through reading and writing is said to be literate in English. One could also be literate in music or in culture, and so forth, as an example of having basic knowledge on which to build more complex information and knowledge. Scientific literacy allows students to understand and appreciate concepts such as climate change, race as an illusion, nuclear energy, and fossil fuels. A revolutionary pedagogy undertakes a profound review of E. D. Hirsch's (1988) notion of cultural literacy,

which leans heavily on European information and facts and not on a multicultural response to knowledge. In an arrogant and monocultural manner, Hirsch promoted, and the school systems accepted, the idea of a "Common Core," which relegated African and Asian information to a background position.

5. *Reasoning.* Reasoning is the ability to determine quantitatively and qualitatively answers based on evidence and facts. Hence, critical thinking and creative communication together allow the student to arrive at conclusions and to present such results adequately and effectively in written or oral form. Reasoning is best when the student understands that calm reflection is necessary to make a studied conclusion before speaking or writing.

SCHOOL ATMOSPHERICS

There is nothing wrong at all with walking into a school building and hearing some low sounds of popular music playing in the background. I would favor classical jazz, but studying the various sounds of music or other sounds, perhaps the voices of birds and the falling of water, to see how children respond might reveal a powerful ethic that school administrators have overlooked. After nearly 20 years of working as a consultant for training teachers how to teach in urban schools, I have concluded that a revolutionary pedagogy works if the entire school system is passionately committed to educating children. This means that principals must commit to helping teachers to make a pedagogical transformation. It should not be necessary to say this, but I have heard enough good teachers lament that they are unable to turn the educational ship around alone with their classes; it must be a districtwide effort. At least in a building, the principal must be dedicated to transformation; one teacher or a group of teachers cannot do it effectively unless the principal buys into the educational transformation.

"Schools are often not about the children but about testing because the bottom line is money," one teacher at an Eastern seaboard school district told me. There are a lot of perceptions tied up in the knot of this statement, and some may be correct and some may be wrong, but one thing is certain—this teacher voices the concern of scores of teachers I have worked with over the years. It is shocking to many teachers when they learn that some superintendents are busy making deals with local businesses, selling off school properties, closing schools to demonstrate to school boards how tough they can be in saving money, and paying millions of dollars for districtwide contracts to a few large testing and curriculum corporations while neglecting programs that will have a lasting impact on the quality of children's education long beyond testing.

The practice of revolutionary pedagogy is a fundamental tool in the creation of a new perspective on education. One cannot take down the entire system while it is still running, just like you cannot close out a national insurance plan when millions of people are invested in it. Revolutionary pedagogy is an incremental process intended to announce the complete overhaul of the educational system. Most American schools do not need tune-ups; they must be introduced to complete overhauls, and that strategy will depend on bold educators.

A revolutionary pedagogy is an intellectual and emotional commitment from school boards and commissions to superintendents and principals. Whole-school buy-ins will raise the profile of any radical cultural program designed to effectively change the school's thermostat, so that principals, teachers, and students, and even cafeteria workers and maintenance people, will know that something different is happening at the school.

Of course, there will be resistance; there is already resistance because those teachers and administrators invested in the current unworkable system of education will not want to change what is comfortable for them, although the system is not working for children. It is my belief that this unworkable system of education is based on modern Western thinking that needs to be corrected to allow for a revolution in pedagogy. To support my position, I can draw on some of the most important contemporary writers on this subject.

For example, Sousa Santos (2007) has positioned the struggle for a proper orientation to knowledge this way:

> Modern Western thinking is an abyssal thinking. It consists of a system of visible and invisible distinctions, the invisible ones being the foundation of the visible ones. The invisible distinctions are established through

radical lines that divide social reality into two realms, the realm of "this side of the line" and the realm of: the other side of the line.

For Sousa Santos, there is this notion that the "other side" becomes non-existent, without reality, in abyssal thinking. Only one side or position is existent: It is the side with the wealth, power, and military. Thus, what is derived from the so-called nonexistent other is neither relevant nor considerable; it is radically excluded and thus beyond the abyss. The most *abysmal* idea about *abyssal* thinking is that there is no possibility of coexistence. When it is educational, it becomes a rampant assertion of a right to exist without others; it is at its source arrogant, supremacist, and war minded. Sousa Santos has restated the problem in a stark manner and has positioned abyssal thinking as the culprit. In this regard, he is correct; it is the inheritance of a dogmatic way of thinking that must be challenged by the new revolutionary pedagogy.

However, let me caution the teachers who are ready to try this revolutionary pedagogy. Administrators tend to lag behind what is going on in the classroom; few of them are revolutionaries themselves because they are so busy socializing to keep their positions that they are afraid to explore what works. The best teachers in a building already know what revolutionary pedagogy is because they are doing it! They have taken the attitude that the core of revolutionary pedagogy is content. They are correct in this assessment because in the end the teacher in the classroom is the educator. They also know that they must not fear their students and indeed must demonstrate the high moral commitment of liking the students. In most cases, administrators were educators, but to educate you must teach, and you cannot be called a good teacher until the pupil has learned. All those people who say they are teachers but have never successfully educated anyone must seriously question their tag as teachers.

Christopher Emdin (2015) speaks of what he calls reality pedagogy. He sees it as an approach to teaching and learning based on youth experiences as the anchor of instruction. There is something positive in this idea, but it is not sufficient. Sometimes the experiences of youth may not lead to appreciation of the complexities and multilevel nature of the social and political context. The danger is that such an individualistic, reality-based pedagogy might emphasize current situations and ideas much more than enduring values. Although one can utilize the immediate cultural styles, one must be careful not to assume that these are transferable to all educational situations. One cannot base pedagogy on one individual but on panoplies of culture. This means that the pedagogy takes into consideration the entire system of the history, politics, social values, and visions of a group of people. The revolutionary pedagogy motto is "Master the culture of your students before you attempt to teach them." I am aware that this is contrary to most educationalist philosophies because they assume that the teacher teaches content alone, but you cannot teach content without an adequate appreciation of the culture of your students.

Revolutionary pedagogy is neither reality pedagogy nor critical pedagogy, although it shares some aspects of both ideas; principally, it is an advance on the teaching and learning in the classroom based on an Afrocentric infusion. In most cases we speak of critical pedagogy as having to do with using concepts that are derived from critical theory in literature and sociology in the field of education. I have been dedicated to some of the key principles of critical pedagogy and in some ways have been influenced by Paulo Freire, Ladson-Billings, and others who see the critical intellectual movement to open up society as necessary and powerful. My main criticism is that you cannot bring something from the category of Western and American literature that is meant to buttress the status quo theorists into the classrooms in urban America and hope to have any real success. To its credit, however, critical pedagogy does bring us closer to the revolutionary idea. In fact, teaching is a political act, as critical pedagogy would contend. However, revolutionary pedagogy is not a variant of critical pedagogy; it may be considered the next phase of the movement for justice. Therefore, the revolutionary pedagogist sees teaching as both a political and a cultural act. Every time teachers stands before a classroom, they are demonstrating either their culture or that of their students. Knowing consciously what we are doing when we are teaching moves this act from a political to a cultural one. When I walk into a classroom and say, "Hotep," I am consciously making a case for the value of an ancient African greeting at the same time as I am teaching the students the oldest greeting in the world. I am asserting my agency; I am being here in the world without apologizing for being. The students see and recognize themselves in this agency. Can you as a teacher learn to do this? Of course, all teachers have the ability to learn information and practices, but it requires not arrogance but humility to see that you do not know all that you need to know to be able to teach these children.

Perhaps more than most other critical theorists, Ladson-Billings, who argued for a culturally relevant pedagogy as early as 1995, knew that something was not quite right with the limited notion of critical theory rooted in European-dominated critiques of capitalist education alone. In fact, she argued that it was significant that many studies of student failure often located "the source of student failure in the nexus of speech and language" (p. 467). Like the revolutionary pedagogists, Ladson-Billings debunked the superficial notion "that Black people don't value education" (p. 467). She says,

> A next step for positing effective pedagogical practices is a theoretical model that not only addresses student achievement but also helps students to accept and affirm their cultural identity while developing critical perspectives that challenge inequities that schools (and other institutions) perpetuate. I term this pedagogy, culturally relevant pedagogy. (p. 469)

I have classified culturally relevant pedagogy as a variant of critical pedagogy with its emphasis on identifying *critical perspectives* that challenge inequities. This may not be entirely appropriate, but it arises from the fact that revolutionary pedagogy is not merely about culture but about culture and agency, and hence the idea is more about the assertion of African or Latin or Asian culture as pedagogically important without necessarily identifying critical perspectives because the assertion of our agency is itself a full critique of any kind of domination. Maulana Karenga (2020) often spoke of a reconstructive system of values, *Kawaida*, which "is an ongoing synthesis of the best of African thought and practice in constant exchange with the world."

CRITICAL PEDAGOGY AND REVOLUTIONARY PEDAGOGY

There are some distinct differences between critical pedagogy and revolutionary pedagogy that are important to understand.

Critical Pedagogy

Critical pedagogy is a philosophy of education that seeks to apply concepts of critical theory to matters of education. Below are the main characteristics of critical pedagogy:

Uses critical theory as a base

Studies cultures to achieve multiculturalism

Advocates teaching as a political act to change the attitudes of students

Looks for social justice to ensure the safety of students (freedom from bullying)

Believes in emancipation from oppression through critical consciousness

Aims to have individuals effect change through social critique and political actions

Revolutionary Pedagogy

Revolutionary pedagogy is a philosophy of education that seeks to overturn ordinary thinking and the methods and practice of creating and delivering knowledge to children by employing Africological, Kemetological, and rhetorical techniques to reset the instructional focus for children. *Africological* refers to the study of African and African American history, cultures, and phenomena from the standpoint of African people as subjects. *Kemetological* refers to the origin of the African narrative in classical Egyptian, that is, Kemetic, society. These ideas are especially centered on radically changing the way urban schools approach instruction. How many schools even use the concept "classical Africa"?

The following are the main characteristics of revolutionary pedagogy:

Uses agency as the central concept for analysis and action; produces culturally diverse methods applicable to highly textured school settings as related to race, gender, and class backgrounds; and realigns the core content to ensure the centrality of the student's culture in the knowledge narrative, whether it is scientific information or value formations based on what activates positive human responses

Suggests the importance of cultural justice as a way to force thinking beyond social justice so that art, music, language, robotics, and all symbol-creating activities can add to the promotion of equality

Reaches for a robust content formula for discipline in the classroom and school building because students are awed by what they do not know but is within their reach

Aims to confirm the transmission of humanizing values based on historical and social narratives that empower the student. If you set the bar high, students will leap over it!

Creating a Revolutionary Pedagogy

The most difficult aspect of creating a revolutionary pedagogy is the resistance on the part of administrators and teachers who are heavily invested in the status quo. They celebrate the current system as if it is the only recourse they have. Of course, this is a mistake and a false understanding of what is required for proper education of children. Thus, for revolutionary pedagogists the *revolution* is about overturning the status quo in the interest of educating children. Our aim as educators is not merely to insert new ideas into the old system but to guarantee that the proper structures, attitudes, philosophy, and orientation are in place for us to be successful transmitters of knowledge. To this end, I have identified five general themes that must be used across the board when we seek to introduce a revolutionary pedagogy. I have stated them as *theses*:

1. There is no universal history with Europe at the center of it. There are only universal responses to the environment and human relations, and those responses have their own nuances and sensitivities based on the circumstances and the people who seek to transmit acquired and learned behaviors to another generation.
2. In the United States, specific educational responses to the transmission of knowledge represent cultural inheritances often complicated by issues of racism, class, and gender. Separating issues so that cultural expressions, historical heritage, and personal inclinations are examined is the best way to affirm revolutionary actions in education.
3. A revolutionary pedagogy begins with a proper corrective at the level of chronology as a feature of place. Without an accurate examination of time and space, it is impossible to understand the need for and the nature of a revolution in the curriculum.
4. Education is the arena of ideological struggle between the status quo and the progressive forces for transformation. To overturn the status quo at the level of curriculum is to go beyond the idea of equity and identity to the transcending of all categories that are rigidly stuck in the cementing ideas of the past to contest the character of a democratic society.

5. A revolutionary pedagogy must necessarily critique and reconstruct the infrastructure of contemporary education if African American, Native American, and Latin American children are to be adequately educated. I believe this will become increasingly important for Asian American children as well when it becomes clear that standardized tests do not indicate adequate revolutionary education. In fact, the growing importance of optional tests for admission to most outstanding colleges means that they are relying on grade point averages and portfolios.

Let me take each one of these theses and explain the concepts as clearly as possible. What is the meaning of "no universal history with Europe at the center?" Well, this should be clear, but I will elaborate on it. European culture represents a particular view of the world; it is not universal, but neither are the views of cultures from Africa or Asia. However, in the contemporary world there has been an emphasis on using Europe as a universal marker. This idea was pushed for a long time by the colonial powers of Europe, which insisted on making the world in the image of Europe. Indians in India were to become Europeans; American Indians, Indigenous Americans, were to become White people with a brown face; and Africans were to become imitators of Europeans to have any value in the modern world.

Second, it is a fact that the requirements of educational systems in the United States have inherited all the biases that exist in the society. Of course, this would be the case in any society where a dominant group of people insist that all education should be based on what they see as constituting the right values, beliefs, attitudes, and gender. To institute a revolutionary pedagogy means that you must be able to crack the code of the sustainable nut of hierarchy, patriarchy, and racism. We know that race is a constructed term used to separate people who are biologically 99.9% the same. Essentially, there is little real difference among *Homo sapiens*.

The third thesis introduces one of the most important elements of revolutionary pedagogy, chronology. I am probably one of the best persons to convey the revolutionary strength in chronology because I really hated the idea of studying dates when I was in high school. Now I am all in because I recognize how dates revolutionized my thinking. How many times have I met people who actually believed that the Parthenon was older than the pyramids? How is it that a teacher was shocked when I told her that Waset was older than Rome and that Inzalo ye Langa was older than Stonehenge? I would not have known myself without study and reflection on the history and significance of Africa in the life of humanity.

I came to the fourth issue from my years of watching one new program after another enter schools. This year, the superintendent is eager to adopt a New Zealand model for curriculum; next year, it is a newly created Swedish program for training students in focusing on their homework; and tomorrow it will be some new project that guarantees perfect attendance by students. I tire of all of this, and you do too, because it is true that, as the eminent professor King (1991) says, "there must be a transformation role for teachers in the curriculum" (p. 135). She emphasizes the use of culture in a positive way as a force in transformative curricula. Our children must have the opportunity to be grounded in African history and culture; otherwise, they will go through hell in their lives even if they pass their courses. These two things are often disconnected, but they do not have to be. Why not know culture and history and become an even better teacher or student because of your foundation in African history?

The last idea is that revolutionary pedagogy engages in a critical review of all the curricula being taught to Black children. Our reviews and critiques must include the humanities, social studies, and all sciences of knowledge, including mathematics and biology, because racism has been insinuated into all aspects of the curriculum. Our children are like guinea pigs in that they are objects of experiments about what can happen if you create structures of knowledge that remind children that they are not represented in human history. So what happens when you teach that mathematics started in Africa? What happens when children know that the first mathematical instruments came from deep inside the African continent?

Since the Afrocentric paradigm was introduced into the philosophical discourse on culture and identity nearly 40 years ago, I proposed Afrocentric education as the principal road to a revolutionary pedagogy and ultimately the total transformation of American education. It was a first step, but it also incorporated the idea that everything was curriculum (Asante, 1991).

Afrocentricity is the process in education that seeks to locate or relocate African people and phenomena within the context of African historical and cultural agency. The key terms would have to be *centeredness, location, marginality, peripheral, location, actors, spectators, de-centeredness, orientation,* and *place* (Asante, 2007; Mazama, 2003). Everyone comes from somewhere, and everyone is going somewhere; we are not disconnected from place, origin, or background.

I was able to use my location as an African born in a racist American society with a history of enslavement of Africans, genocide of Native peoples, and dispossession of Mexicans as an initial source for the overturning of a Eurocentric hegemony that imposed its will on all forms of knowledge and on all people as a conquering ideology. If the education of dispossessed people cannot produce conquest over malice and racism, then that education is a failure. If White students who are in school cannot be taught the common humanity of the people of the earth, then their education is essentially useless for the world they will confront.

What is the difference between Afrocentricity and Africanity? Africanity refers to the customs and styles of culture often followed in terms of food, festivals, music, and language. Afrocentricity is a much more conscious activity, one that depends on knowledge and will. One can practice Africanity without having any concern for transforming education or anything else; however, the Afrocentrist looks at the pedagogical condition and asks, "How can we improve the agency of Blacks in this or that narrative?" Since historiography is a method of writing narratives of phenomena and people, "how can one write about Africans without giving them the subject place in narratives of Africa?"

Afrocentricity is not a counterpart to Eurocentricity as it is seen in the United States and Europe. There have been several important critiques of Eurocentricity. Nevertheless, there is still a tendency for someone to say, "Well, Afrocentricity is Eurocentricity in dark face." Whenever I hear such a comment, I know full well that the person has never read anything written by a serious scholar on Afrocentricity. While Eurocentricity tends to operate as an ethnocentric concept, assuming that European ways are universal and therefore superior, this is unthinkable in Afrocentricity. Indeed, rather than a counterpart to this type of thinking, Afrocentricity is a definite *counterpoint.*

On the other hand, Afrocentricity is not the opposite of Eurocentricity (Asante, 1987). In fact, Afrocentricity does not valorize itself while degrading other perspectives. Eurocentricity imposes its view as universal, making a particular historical reality the sum, in the European's view, of the human experience (Asante, 1991). It is based on White supremacist notions that endeavor to protect white advantage in education, economics, and politics by teaching that what is white is universal, even human. On the other hand, Eurocentric instruction often de-valorizes what is Black, or African. Here, the words of Goodwin (2010)—renowned teacher and innovative leader of the Teacher Center in Rochester, New York—are important when she writes,

> Centering Black people in this discussion about educating Black children and their community brings culture, history, worldview, and ontology from the margins of importance to the foreground of required learning for teacher educators, teachers, policy makers, and the Black community. (p. 1)

Furthermore, what are the implications for education if the teacher does not understand how to raise questions about the writing of history itself? Here is where the philosophy of writing, historiography, makes an entry to allow us to ask who developed the questions, who answers the questions, and what is the purpose of the questions in the first place?

Approaches to Revolutionary Pedagogy

Afrocentricity seeks to place the African in the center of events and situations that involve African people. Why should Africans be on the periphery of their own narrative? Why should anyone dictate the narratives of knowledge or power or origin of others? Thus, the act of moving Africans to the center of their own historical narrative. with all of its attendant intellectual baggage, is an Afrocentric act. Using the idea of paradigm, Mazama (2003) sought to advance Afrocentricity as a transformative engine for every aspect of African life, that is, religion, education, politics, development, and culture.

Africology is the Afrocentric study of African phenomena transgenerationally and transcontinentally.

Although I believe that the Afrocentrist is closest to the revolutionary pedagogist, I recognize Afrocentricity as a stepping-stone to a more holistic way of grappling with a diverse student population in a hetero-geneous, advanced technological society. Only Afrocentrists, and possibly the Asiocentrists Yoshitaka Miike and Jing Yin, have reached the bridge across the chasm to revolutionary pedagogy because they have seen that it is not enough to "decolonize" Western education but one must also act to create an ethic of revolutionary instruction. They used the so-called fortune cookie to show the intrusion of the West into something that was supposed to be Chinese (Yin & Miike, 2008). It is impossible for Eurocentrists, especially the critical pedagogical school thinkers, to make the necessary changes because they are locked into the formula where Europe is always the teacher and the others are the students. For them, critical work rarely, if ever, involves criticism of Eurocentrism; it is rather a critique of liberal democracies. They do not see Europe alongside oth-ers but rather as a neoliberal tendency that could encapsulate everybody else. Miike (2007) explored this idea in communication theory and research and argued for a much broader perspective on communication. The liberation of Eurocentrists from the need to seek hegemony will be one of the major liberations of the 21st century. One reason why multi-culturalism came to an end is the insistence on the part of some that the Eurocentric model afforded a "chance" for everyone to stand under the umbrella held by Europe. A rejection of this paternal attitude is a blow for a more revolutionary approach to culture than what we have inher-ited from the critical pedagogical school.

Given the overwhelmingly horrendous social policies of our society, there is every reason for social justice to be a fundamental pursuit of all sectors of society. Yet cultural justice as represented in archives of memory, sym-bols of success, artistic values, and dramatic genius must be placed before our children as examples of science, art, culture, and philosophy.

I should be able to walk into any school and see an image of Imhotep, builder of the first pyramid, on the walls of the school. A series of paint-ings or photographs of Yenenga, Yaa Asantewaa, Hatshepsut, Amanishakete, Nandi, Queen Tiye and Nehanda should adorn the school building and classrooms alongside the more popular images of Martin Luther King Jr., Malcolm X, Harriet Tubman, Frederick Douglass, W. E. B. Du Bois, and Fannie Lou Hamer. Children should be surrounded by the heroes who fought for justice in all of its forms. I would like to see a corner for the astrophysicists and astronauts, the poets and novelists, the award-winning dramatists, dancers, and choreographers, the philosophers and educational innovators—a veritable festival of talent should stare down at students at every turn. This is what revolutionary education looks like on the walls of a school building.

There have been many attempts by many municipalities and several states to bring a more equitable approach to education. In New Jersey, outstanding legislators Assemblymen William Payne and Craig A. Stanley proposed one of the more significant movements in the nation. It was called the Amistad Bill, named for the ship *Amistad*, which was taken over by Sengbe and other Africans intended for slavery.

The objective of the bill was to recognize the integral part African Americans have played at every turn in this nation's history. The Amistad Bill (A1301), which became law in 2002, directed New Jersey schools to incorporate African American history into their social studies curriculum. This legislation also created the Amistad Commission, a 23-member body charged with ensuring that African American history is adequately taught in the state's classrooms.

Furthermore, Payne and Stanley called on the Amistad Commission to ensure that there would be materials and texts that could integrate African contributions into the curriculum. They suggested three principal goals:

1. To infuse the history of Africans and African Americans into the social studies curriculum in order to provide an accurate, complete, and inclusive history
2. To ensure that New Jersey teachers are equipped to effectively teach the revised social studies core curriculum content
3. To create and coordinate workshops, seminars, institutes, memorials, and events that raise public awareness about the importance of the history of African Americans to the growth and development of American society in the global context

Leading in New Jersey in implementing the Amistad Bill was Union County Schools, including towns such as Rahway and Rosedale. Almost as soon as the bill was enacted, local activists in Rahway embraced the idea and pressured the superintendent to introduce a program for training teachers in African American history. What the Amistad Bill highlighted was the need to create a revolutionary pedagogy that would address issues of culture. Unfortunately, by 2022, the Amistad Bill in New Jersey had lost most of its ambition to transform the teaching of African American history in schools.

Given the need to re-center historiography, the revolutionary pedagogy I suggest will seek to undermine notions of universalism and globalization that are not inclusive. All talk of the mainstream without Africa, or globalization that dismisses the African and Asian worlds must be abandoned. No longer can we or must we as educators be held hostages to a system of education that is meant to destroy motivation and to reduce our children to automatons.

I resent the premise on which the current educational system is based because it assumes that something is wrong with African American children. Grounded in the doctrine of European supremacy, the educational system promotes a monocultural insistence on education that reduces all other cultural expressions to footnotes or pop-ups.

Goodwin (2010) has captured one of the reasons for a lack of serious concern about the practice of pedagogy from an Afrocentric perspective. She says, "The refusal to include Afrocentric theorists as significant participants in responding to the failure of urban school districts to effectively educate Black children is a central part of the cultural denial, violence, and domination experienced by African descent communities" (p. 7). I believe that Goodwin has struck a chord that is central to the lack of diverse thinking about pedagogy. As I see it, Afrocentrists have raised the most fundamental questions about the educational system. They alone seem to understand that it is not enough to discuss the cultural idea without devoting extensive space and time to the question of changing the entire premise on which we place culture. One cannot simply add Latin, African, and Native American, and Asian information into the white bottle and shake it up and get what is necessary for all students. The bottle must be changed, and all information must be shared from all bottles equally and poured into a new vessel. This is revolutionary; all else is nothing but domination.

Our challenges are great because so long as urban schools remain unchanged it is unthinkable that the achievement of low–economic background children will improve regardless of their culture or racial origins. Also, as long as the curriculum is dependent on testing that is designed to identify students for different levels of attention, the gulf between the classes will continue to grow. Giving all students proper esteem will help elevate the thinking of students in the classroom regardless of their class, gender, or cultural background.

CHAPTER 2

The Problem With American Education

In June 2016, Liz Sablich wrote an article illustrating the racial disparities in American education. The point that was made resonates with me: Education is never a major part of the conversation on racial inequalities in the United States. Even when significant experts, such as those at the Brookings Institution, highlight issues that reflect disparities, we are still left with limited appreciation of the depth of racism in the system. Therefore, in some respects, Afrocentrists have argued for a completely revolutionary approach to the question of education. They recognize that the problem is not race necessarily but racism, which is deeply entrenched in our thinking and buried in the soil and in the souls of the most liberal teachers.

The American nation has rarely dealt openly with the disenfranchisement of African Americans. From the end of the Civil War until the beginning of the 21st century, we have had conflicted policy on the education of Black children. When the First Mohonk Conference on the Negro Question was held on June 4–6, 1890, A. K. Smiley quoted from a speech that had been given by former U.S. president Rutherford B. Hayes in relationship to the Conferences on the Indian:

> I will not attempt to say more; but so gratified am I with what I have seen of the methods and of the spirit of this Mohonk Conference that I cannot

but hope that the day may soon come when that other weaker race, not of a quarter of a million, but of six million, shall have some such annual assembly as this to consider its condition and to aid it to rise to the full stature of true American citizenship. (Barrows, 1890, p. 3)

After some discussion, Hayes was elected chair of the Mohonk Conference on the Negro Question, and among other things, he said,

Every Christian, will surely be persuaded that the American people have a grave and indispensable duty to perform with respect to the millions of men and women among our countrymen whose ancestors our fathers brought from Africa to be held in bondage here in America. It may be justly said in the deepest sense of the words, that we are indeed the keepers of "our brothers in black." We are responsible for their presence and condition on this continent. Having deprived them of their labor, liberty, and manhood, and grown rich and strong while doing it we have no excuse for neglecting them, if our selfishness prompted us to do so. But, in truth, their welfare and ours, if not one and the same, are inseparable. These millions who have been so cruelly degraded must be lifted up, or we ourselves will be dragged down. (Barrows, 1890, p. 4)

Clearly, there was significant concern about the condition of millions of Africans in the American nation who did not have the same possibilities as whites. In fact, Hayes was right in his understanding of the situation. He said,

In the Southern States are seven millions of colored people, of whom probably one-half are unable to read and write; and illiteracy in their case, we are told, means far more than ignorance of letters. It means a condition, according to a high authority, "compounded of ignorance, superstition, shiftlessness, vulgarity, and vice." There may be gross exaggerations in the tales we hear of the Voodoo paganism, which, under the name of religion, lurks, if it does not prevail, in the cotton and cane growing districts of the South known as the black belt. (Barrows, 1890, p. 5)

Hayes had not performed well in regard to Africans when he was in the White House, and there is no doubt in my mind that this gnawed at whatever sense of decency he still held after his presidency. He had come into office after a deal made with the devil, so to speak, because he had served in the Union Army and had supported the freedom of Africans from bondage but to become president had to succumb to the demand of the South to remove the soldiers from the rebellious states. In 1876, Hayes contested one of the most contentious elections in American history. He lost the official popular vote to the White racist Samuel J. Tilden because the southern states suppressed the southern Black votes as well as the votes of the White Republicans working in the South. Hayes won a hotly contested fight in the electoral college after a congressional commission gave him 20 of the contested electoral votes. The result was the Compromise of 1877, in which the southern Democrats acquiesced to Hayes's election and the president withdrew the remaining U.S. troops protecting the freed Africans and Republican office holders in the South. Former president Ulysses S. Grant had removed the soldiers from Florida, and Hayes completed the job in South Carolina and Louisiana. When the army troops left their camps, many White Republicans, people from the party of Lincoln who had come to assist the Africans, also left the South. Black people felt betrayed by the White liberals who ran back to the North as soon as the protection was gone, leaving us to the vagaries, vices, and victimizations of the Ku Klux Klan and any other distorted-minded white. Soon, White southerners dominated the governments in the southern states.

After leaving the presidency, Hayes took on a Jimmy Carter–like position of one seeking to do the justice that he had neither the political power nor the political will to do while he was president. Yet it must be said to his credit that he saw the problem from the same side as the evidence. A population exploited for nearly 250 years, with untold masses who never saw a day of freedom, abused under the sun and through the night, whipped in the morning and the evening, and freed without property or proper protection, stood in the midst of an American nation built on the backs of this people, who were without education, psychological grounding in culture, or material wealth. Yet the only solution that could be proffered was the Booker T. Washington plan for educating the hands and hearts of Blacks to make them better servants for whites. Washington's philosophy was a major factor in the room with the attendees, though his name does not appear on the official list of those present. Yet his dynamic presentation of Black people as willing and capable servants of the white nation, educated in the ways of hands and hearts, was unmistakably present. In fact, this was the only solution that made sense to the leading whites in the nation. They were not about to educate Blacks to compete with whites; they could support industrial education that would make Blacks better workers for white interests. Consequently, neither Black children nor White children were properly educated. While Blacks received education that was inferior in content and context, whites received the doctrine of white supremacy in education because they were "better" than Blacks in their minds. Whites had newer school buildings, the newest books, and the most qualified teachers, and White parents figured that since their taxes were paying for the schools, they "deserved" the better schools; after all, they were white. We have inherited this inequality even in an era of integration.

It should not be possible in a democratic nation for a child to attend school and after 10 or 12 years leave school with attitudes like those of Dylann Roof, the Charleston, South Carolina, shooter who wanted to start a race war. What proper education would lead four young Black adults to abuse a young mentally disabled White man while shouting racial epithets at him? Of course, I recognize that schools cannot do everything, but education, as its principal purpose, should make a difference in how students are socialized. What are we teaching if children persist in being bigots after we have taught them? What are we teaching?

This is not the end of the matter. Neither should it be possible that school readiness for Black children is eternally behind that of White children. In fact, Sean Reardon and Ximena Portilla (2016) said that between 1998 and 2010 the black–white gap in school readiness was indistinguishable from zero but where there was any perceived change there may have been several factors.

> There are a number of reasons to suspect that racial/ethnic and income school readiness gaps might have changed from 1998 to 2010, including changes in the income distribution (including changes in racial income disparities), changes in parental investments in children, changes in residential segregation, changes in preschool enrollment patterns, and changes in social policies that affect children.

We have a severe problem when a certain evocative mendacity covers every interpretation of what's wrong with the system.

I cannot accept the educational status quo in either elementary or secondary schools in America. I can neither accept nor appreciate the structure and scope of the curriculum in most universities. Consequently, I am forced by circumstances to be against the status quo, to seek its overthrow, to obliterate its racist ethic, and to demand a new vision of education for all children. Christopher Emdin (2015) has written an insightful book for whites teaching in urban areas, but this book could just as well have been written for Blacks teaching Black children. It seems that even Black teachers, who were taught by White teachers in school or college, have forgotten how to teach African American children based on the current reality. My contention is that if you cannot teach children from the most depressed areas of American cities, then you should not call yourself a teacher. Most people calling themselves teachers would have little difficulty teaching children from their own socioeconomic and racial background; the real test comes when you have to teach children who do not reflect your community or values. Lisa Delpit's (1995/2006) dictum on teaching other people's children is quite appropriate because it is essential that we teach other people's children as we would teach our own.

Black children who are punished for aggressive behavior, not *violence*, are not regarded as leaders but as troublemakers in most academic circles. The same behavior by White students might mark them for leadership and future potential to be successful. While some people have seen this as an economic differential, which it might be as well, I find racial animus in the way teachers, White, Black, Asian, or Latinx, treat African American children who demonstrate noncognitive abilities that are said to be predictive, in some cases, of success in later life. One can examine the work of economist Nicholas Papageorge on this issue. Papageorge was interested in the demographic relationship between teachers and students (Gershenson et al., 2016).

Why is it that White teachers have lower expectations for Black children? I remember that when I was in elementary and high school in Nashville, Tennessee, my teachers all felt I would be successful. My teachers, with the exception of one, Mr. Brent, were all Black. They did not approach Black children with a lower educational or academic vision than we had for ourselves. This is why the research shows that non-Black teachers usually have lower academic expectations for African American students than Black teachers. We also know that the more often a Black student is paired with a Black teacher the less likely that student is suspended from school. White teachers tend to suspend Black students much more than Black teachers.

Schools typically have tracking toward more advanced classes for students who live in white or Asian neighborhoods and less advanced classes are offered to qualified students who are African American or Latin American. These are decisions that are interwoven into the mythology of expectations, and they significantly lower the opportunities for children in urban areas.

In an unequal system, African American children earn diplomas and college degrees to a lesser extent than white and Asian children, thus augmenting the deep trenches already left by the tracking system. With graduation rates at the high school level and the college level significantly lower than those of their counterparts, African American and Latin American students are often well on the road toward second-tier standing in the society. In no society that prides itself on democracy and equal opportunity will this situation be tolerable; it demands a revolutionary approach to education and to pedagogy.

CLASS AND RACE

If you show me a school in America where 75% of the children live below the poverty line, I will show you a low-performing school. There are no miracles here, only the terrain of class and race. Some principals know that when they are given low-performing schools and asked to "turn them around" they are being set up for failure. There are a few who do not fail, but for the most part any school that has 75% of its students coming from families that live below the poverty level will have lower test scores. On the other hand, richer school districts do better on tests.

I am one of the first to admit that everything cannot be pinned on economics, but I still insist that economics is a major player in the arena of testing. Evidence shows that this is the case. It may be, for example, that children whose parents participate in the school program do better on tests and in behavior. So school participation is an important factor for school success, but lack of participation is sometimes tied to the economic level of the parents.

So the challenge for the principal and the teacher is how to break the chain of economics so that the child will be free to learn. Here is where revolutionary pedagogy enters the picture with some ideas. You can intervene in this situation on two levels: (1) school level and (2) teacher level.

At the school level, the principal must make the school a virtual home for the children so that it becomes an idealized version of the most beautiful Afrocentric home possible. In Detroit, a principal at such a school once told me that it was hard to get the children to leave the school because they did not want to go home; the school had become home to them, and they appreciated its beauty, comfort, and colors! It was cheerful, not drab. The school gave them snacks after the classes were over. They were rewarded for good behavior and had various types of awards for academics and behavior.

The teacher level is much more nuanced. There are two teacher qualities that Mario Root, a super-successful school counselor at Bishop Dunn High School in Dallas, Texas, shared with me. When I was interviewing administrators about ideal teachers, Root told me that the best teachers are those who have high standards and empathy at the same time. He said that a teacher could have high standards and no empathy, and that teacher would never reach the category of an outstanding teacher. However, if a teacher only had empathy and no high standards, then students would take advantage of that teacher and never be motivated to succeed. He emphasized that the outstanding teacher has high standards *and* empathy.

I did not understand Root to mean that the teacher had to have high standards as in strict, rigid rules but rather high expectations of the students. Most students can see through the behavior and attitude of teachers quite easily. A teacher armed with revolutionary pedagogy sentiments will walk into the classroom with high expectations for the least of the students. I like to say to my classes, "You all have A grades today; tomorrow depends upon you." Sometimes I also tell the class, "I believe in you and know that you can get an A grade in this class. Nothing is in your way but your own efforts. I will work with you if you work with me." Students see this as an opening for them to do well, and they know that if they do not do well, the teacher will assist them to the limit of what is possible.

On the other hand, empathy allows the teacher to identify with the emotions, values, and mental state of the student. It is not possible for a teacher to know every child's situation, but the teacher might be able to discover that a student has special problems by having a chat with the student when he or she is not performing well. In one high school in Philadelphia, the teacher discovered that a student was getting to class late because she had to prepare breakfast for her two younger siblings as the father had to return to Hong Kong for work for several weeks. Although only a freshman in high school, this young girl was responsible for two siblings' food and dress in the mornings. For the teacher to not know these circumstances may mean that the teacher places undue stress on herself and the student by insisting that the student is a poor student. Empathy is not simply feeling about a student's situation but wanting the student to succeed so deeply that you show empathy. I typically ask students to tell me about their families, how they are doing, whether they are happy to be in class, and whether they have time to work at home. Establishing empathy may not change the student's grade but it is more likely to give the teacher a deeper insight into the situation than otherwise.

THE PERILS OF ADMINISTRATIVE DECISIONS

One of the worst problems faced by revolutionary pedagogy practitioners is dealing with incompetent superintendents and top administrators. They are often some of the biggest impediments to the implementation of strategies that will help students succeed. The incompetence of these administrators is not mean spirited; it is just ignorance of how to educate children. There are several reasons for this condition. In the first place, you do not have to know anything about African American culture to be a superintendent, and yet when you become a leader in the larger school districts, you will be confronted with the question of what to do with the lowest-achieving schools in the poorer neighborhoods. Those schools are typically in areas with the largest Black populations. Nevertheless, superintendents when offered opportunities to assist their teachers, who are mostly white, in preparing to teach the children in these low-performing schools have a problem spending money to make the necessary changes. Teachers are not well educated when it comes to the culture of children, and they rarely know how to approach children who do not have the same culture as theirs. They actually need help, which is not provided in any school of education that I know because one has to know both African American culture and education. Second, administrators are often chasing the business end of the school job, so they lose sight, if they ever had it, of the goal of providing the best education for the largest number of students. In most districts, if the lowest-achieving schools were assisted, the districts would overcome more than a third of their problems with achievement. Third, the school culture has a bad testing problem. This multibillion-dollar industry has seduced most of the school districts in the United States. Testing and evaluating children on how quickly they can answer a series of questions is now considered the best way to decide how to track students. Of course, this teaching to tests has almost nothing to do with learning, and administrators have figured out that school boards and state administrators do not want to hear anything about culture or pedagogy, only about test scores. This is of great peril to African American children.

I have faced this problem in several districts, including Pittsburgh and Kansas City. The Pittsburgh case is classic. The Equity and Diversity Committee, the Board of Education, and the superintendent asked me to come speak to administrators and teachers about creating a program for ensuring students' success. The program developed by me and Ama Mazama had been implemented for only six months when the district brought in another superintendent because of the retirement of the previous one. The new superintendent moved as quickly as possible, but awkwardly, to take down all of the programs of his predecessor, a common but fateful decision when administrations change. The fact that he had come into the district under a cloud of suspicion about fudging his resume did not help the situation. Psychologically, he probably felt that he had to prove himself as a person who had higher standards than the previous administrator and therefore could not support a serious revolutionary pedagogy that asserted an Afrocentric educational training for teachers; he had to stand only for testing and evaluation standards. This was not only a mistake, it had no possibility of succeeding as a strategy for helping the mass of students in the district, leave alone the ones at the lowest end in the testing game. Scores only change when students are motivated to learn. Students are motivated to learn when they have teachers who are transformative in their pedagogy.

The Kansas City problem was not so much that the superintendent was not committed to doing something; it was that he had not put in place any assertive Afrocentric administrators around him to insist that the schools conduct the Afrocentric training as planned. The superintendent failed to oversee the principals in the two Afrocentric schools, and they operated on their own, with no guidance and no understanding of what it meant to be leaders of Afrocentric schools. If a principal cannot define Afrocentricity, then that person has no business being around an Afrocentric school. But then again, a superintendent often gives in to the community that is demanding an Afrocentric school, because it knows this is correct, and loses sight of the revolutionary nature of this pedagogy. A true Afrocentric school has at its core a revolutionary pedagogy that emphasizes the agency of African Americans in their own narrative as well as the expansion of social justice.

Overcoming the peril of weak superintendents of schools will have to be the job of the best school board members and community members, those committed to fighting for children despite the incompetence, especially the cultural incompetence, of superintendents.

SUCCESS DEPENDS ON LOVING
THE STUDENT'S CULTURE

A long train of educators and lovers of culture precede this generation. Women particularly elevated the teaching profession with revolutionary goals. Nannie Helen Burroughs stood on the shoulders of Anna Julia

Cooper and Mary Church Terrell. Like those women of the public spaces and the private strategy meetings, Burroughs took to the life of education, starting a National Training School to bring about an uplift in the African American community around the issues of wage earning, discipline, and making the best of difficult situations. Burroughs did not turn her dark face away from trouble; she, like millions of others, ran directly toward trouble as a guardian of the race because she knew and loved the people. White teachers who want to be successful must love their students' culture as they love their own, wanting to know more, to understand more, and to listen with an empathetic ear. Administrators who reward teachers must learn to recognize these genuine revolutionary pedagogists.

Just as we have bad administrators, we have had some exceptionally gifted administrators. One of the best to live in the United States was the courageous and brilliant Barbara Sizemore. She was the first African American woman to head a major school district as superintendent when she was hired by Washington, D.C., in 1973. The defining characteristic of Sizemore was her fierce determination to see Black children succeed despite the negative reputation of urban schools. However, her willingness to challenge the status quo and to project the will to raise the standards for teachers who taught Black children put her in direct confrontation with the old guard of the Washington, D.C., elected school board. They fired Sizemore in 1975, and she went on to become a leading university administrator of education. The *Washington Post* wrote,

> Mrs. Sizemore assumed center stage in an arena that was wracked by social ferment, political battles and court fights during the two decades of civil rights struggles and the District's drive for home rule. The campaign for self-government ended only last year with the city's first elected mayor and Council in more than a century. (Lamb, 2004)

Calling her "insubordinate," a term used frequently in reference to Blacks with a strong personality in the 1970s, the school board said essentially that they could not control her. She refused to resign and so these elected agents of the status quo had to fire her.

I have always considered Sizemore as one of the educational outliers in the sense that she was interested in raising the academic achievement of African American students because she knew that African American students could learn anything any other students could learn, and so she stirred controversy when she said in a speech that she had "a higher calling than educating children, and that was uplifting my race" (Lamb, 2004). In an interview with the *Washington Post* in 1975, she said, "I did not understand that in order to be superintendent of schools I was to give up my higher mission" (Lamb, 2004). Her impact was electric throughout the nation as progressives flocked to her side and made her a star in the educational arena. Perhaps her greatest champion was the professor of education at Howard University, Nancy Arnez, who claimed that Sizemore was ahead of her time. Arnez authored a case study, *The Besieged Superintendent* (1981), which stated that Sizemore could stand up to authority and do things that others would not even try. Arnez told *Education Week* in 1996 that Sizemore's approach to Congress was not one of supplication but one of advocating for nonachieving students. She had made her mind up that she would do all that was in her power to transform the school district. This is a legacy of a prototypical revolutionary pedagogy.

Barbara Sizemore

About the same time as Sizemore was making her insightful observations about the schooling of Black children, Adelaide L. Sanford was championing Black children as a principal in New York City. She was born in Brooklyn on November 27, 1925, and earned a B.Ed. at Brooklyn College in 1947. She received her M.Ed. degree from Wellesley College in 1950 and then taught in elementary schools in New York until 1965. When she was hired as an assistant principal, she was able to see the educational process up close as an administrator would see it. By 1967, she had her doctorate from Fordham University and soon became principal of Crispus Attucks School in Brooklyn, where her style of leadership and powerful ethic of loving the children to motivate them to do better became the hallmark of her career. She taught her students to embrace their African heritage or whatever their background happened to be. This was, but should not have been, revolutionary to promote excellence and dynamic achievement. She defended her students and her faculty and soon became a household name and a national icon in the African American community of educators, reaching the enviable position of Queen Mother in the mythology of African American communities. This title is bestowed informally on women leaders who shoulder the responsibility of nurturing an entire community with their love and wisdom. It may be something unknown in other American communities, but it is quite significant among African Americans, following in the tradition of Queen Mother Moore—the legendary African American woman born in Louisiana who stood up in a meeting in New Orleans where Marcus Garvey was speaking and shouted to the police and others who wanted to interrupt, "Let Garvey speak! Let Garvey speak!"—who moved to Harlem, New York, and became a leader of the Universal Negro Improvement Association and other organizations, including the Universal Association of Ethiopian Women, and then in 1972 was given the title of Queen Mother by the Asante people of Ghana. Her battles for civil rights and systematic nationalism as well as the Garvey incident seared her name and charismatic style into African American culture. Other women would have that charisma and be accorded the title of Queen Mother as well, and one of the greatest is Sanford, who received her title before she joined the New York State Board of Regents for Education. Queen Mother Sanford has been cited by many scholars and educators for her courage and brilliance. Author Fred Monderson wrote about her in three of his books because of her solidarity with the African American community. In his book *Ladies in the House*, Monderson (2013) celebrates the history of African women who have demonstrated an undying love of culture; Sanford is such a woman.

In 1986, Sanford won unanimous election to the Board of Regents of the State University of New York. As chairperson of the Regents' Committee on Low Performing Schools, she worked to shape new, culturally relevant educational policies to close the gap in student performance among schools. Reflecting her community and her love of African traditions and style, Sanford became known as the voice of African American students and teachers, and her eloquence and impeccable African dresses brought her a larger-than-life reputation as a fearless and courageous person who was never crude or rude in her statements on issues or recommendations for solutions. Alongside serving as a regent, Sanford taught at Baruch College and Fordham University.

Many honors and awards were bestowed on Sanford for her work; she received the Congressional Black Caucus Foundation's humanitarian award, and distinguished alumna awards from Wellesley College and Brooklyn College. In addition, she was named one of the HistoryMakers, a group of less than 10,000 African Americans who are considered world-class citizens of culture and success in all fields of science, art, and education.

Sanford played an instrumental role in creating the John Henrik Clarke House in Harlem, dedicated to African history, African American culture, and promotion of the brilliant work of the late historian John Henrik Clarke. The Clarke House continues Sanford's creative approach to education, including education of the masses of people who visit it for lectures.

I once had the chance of witnessing Sanford's magic as she spoke to the Rochester, New York, Teachers Union, and when she had completed her brief talk, no more than 15 minutes, I was moved to ask permission to say a few words. When Susan Goodwin, the moderator, said that I could speak. I remember speaking extemporaneously and saying,

> What words can convey the intellect, grace, and beauty of a natural-born queen? I only know that when one is in Adelaide's presence, with her large, inviting smile that embraces her children, her people, it is as if one is in the presence of the origin of awe. So today, to be warmed by her sun is magnificent because her knowledge of education and love of inner-city children suggest radiance beyond the ordinary.

I took my seat to the applause of the audience, who shared my own sentiments. We had seen up close the dance of a master teacher and felt blessed by her steady sense of purpose and eternal optimism about the future of education.

Sanford's trip to Vicksburg, Mississippi, as a small child had a profound impact on her. After her mother's car had been forced off the road and into a ditch, Sanford's mother soon found herself fending off prosecution from a racist judge and enduring a surgical procedure for an injury without anesthesia. Talking to Sanford about this incident, one can see that she developed an intense hatred of racism and inequality and knew that the obstacles placed in the way of Black children often went right back to racist attitudes that saw Black children as less than White children. She vowed to break the back of this kind of racism in education wherever she could. Her unyielding belief in the capacity of Black children to succeed was often met with skepticism and roadblocks. Her efforts to gain quality education facilities for Black children extended to workers as well. After prolonged confrontations with New York mayor Robert Wagner, Sanford led the effort to ensure that Black laborers were able to work on school construction projects throughout the city of New York. After all, what we discovered was that one could not separate educational equity from general equity; what confronted teachers and students in the educational sector were problems like the ones found in other sectors.

All people, in every country and of every nation, have identified individuals who deserve to be celebrated and praised for the work that they are doing and have done. The names of Harriet Tubman, Garvey, Zumbi, Queen Tiye, Nehanda, Toussaint L'Ouverture, Dessalines, Fannie Lou Hamer, Abdias Nascimento, Nat Turner, Yanga, and a thousand others sing out from the panoply of heaven that we are witnesses to a profound living giant who walks among us.

Sanford came into the world, as it announced her, as a child of Africa. Her resistance to the oppression of our children; her incredible defense of African American culture as a teacher, as a principal, and while sitting on the New York Board of Regents for Education; and her masterful teaching techniques have honored the fighting educators beyond words.

Haki and Safisha Madhubuti opened one of the first African American networks of charter schools in 1998.

The network, under the name Betty Shabazz International Charter Schools, includes the Betty Shabazz Academy (Grades K–8), Barbara A. Sizemore Academy (Grades K–8), and DuSable Leadership Academy (Grades 9–12). Betty Shabazz was named for the wife of Malcolm X, and DuSable was named for the African, probably of Haitian origin, who was the first settler in Chicago, Illinois. Barbara Sizemore Academy was named after the former Washington school superintendent, the first African American woman to lead a major school system. The network of schools consistently produced exemplary, high-achieving students with a profoundly deep understanding of and appreciation for their cultural identity and a desire to make the community better. So the schools gained reputations for instilling pride, motivation, and a sense of purpose in the children. However, like other Afrocentric charter schools, the famed Chicago schools have found it difficult to teach their students to score well on standardized tests. In fact, Martell Teasley wrote in the *Journal of African American Studies* in January 2016 that the two dozen Afrocentric charters he examined fell short of the national testing standards. Teasley said that he supported the concept and mission of the schools but they needed to prepare all students for the standardized tests. Without that, he said, African-centered schools will fail to earn mainstream legitimacy and will be soft targets for school boards looking to make budget cuts (Teasley et al., 2016).

The rise of consciousness during the 1960s was partly ushered in by poet Don L. Lee, who became Haki Madhubuti, and Carol D. Lee, who became Safisha Madhubuti. After founding Third World Press and the Institute for Positive Education, Safisha earned a doctorate and became a professor of education and social policy at Northwestern University. Haki, already a famous poet, became an administrator and publisher. They have become a legendary couple in the movement for Afrocentric schools.

Freya Anderson Rivers is a direct intellectual and educational descendant of Sizemore and a consistent exponent of Sanford's style of determination but with a more robust philosophical perspective on what has to be done for African American children. Sizemore's attitude and general sense of what was wrong with the system were exceptionally astute, but Rivers took the issue to another level and proposed to create the type of school that was necessary to overcome the narratives of failure. Thus, when she created Sankofa Shule in Lansing, Michigan, she was seeking to introduce an Afrocentric infusion into a charter school. After leaving Sankofa Shule, Rivers went on to establish one of the most important Afrocentric infusion consulting groups in the nation, the Genius Academy, with Julian Brooks, Lamailede Assata Moore, Shariba Rivers, and Angie Hawkins-Rivers. Sankofa Shule was called an "educational powerhouse" by *U.S. News and World Report* because Freya Rivers, as superintendent and founder, refused to believe the myths about Black students. She had received her B.S. from Louisiana State University, an M.Ed. from Southern University, and a doctorate from Vanderbilt University. Rivers overlaid every aspect of Sankofa Shule with assertive African cultural images, motifs, cultural ideas, and values.

It is tempting to speak of Rivers as a person with an enormous, more than 35 years of educational experience and use this as a justification for her success, but this is only half correct. Many educators work in the field for 30, 40, and even 50 years without ever understanding the significance of a centered education for students. Therefore, I say that Rivers had an active intellectual curiosity about the educational system itself, which allowed her to make a powerful demonstration of what African American students could achieve. I was her history and cultural consultant when she took 40 African American elementary children to Egypt to see the pyramids built by Africans in Africa! We took them to the villages of contemporary Black Egyptians, the descendants of the builders of the temples and tombs, and saw how inspired these students were and how reciprocal was the feeling of the Egyptians. Young children who could read Japanese, kiSwahili, and Middle Egyptian stunned the elders in Egypt and those who came along as chaperones. It is rare that we see change agents as brilliant as Rivers, whose demonstration of teaching with and for excellence inspired a generation of educators. In effect, Rivers found her voice in education because of the courage of her father, Dr. Dupuy H. Anderson, who was a local human rights fighter in Baton Rouge, Louisiana. Anderson had sent her to school in Baton Rouge in the 1950s as part of the grand attack on segregated schools in the South. In her memoir, *Swallowed Tears*, Rivers (2012) points to her father as one of the central influences in her life because he persisted in creating change despite threats on his life. This experience steeled Rivers against all obstacles to properly educating African American students.

The revolutionary pedagogist often appears in the classroom unbeknownst to the school superintendent but is well known to the principal and the students in the classroom. This was the case with Christine Thomas Wiggins, who taught at Martin Luther King High School and

Morris E. Leeds Middle School in Philadelphia, Pennsylvania for 12 years. During that time, Wiggins proved to be one of the most outstanding teachers in these schools. At Leeds, she made a major contribution to the infusion of African American content in the lesson plans of the school. Her teacher colleagues were impressed with Wiggins's dedication to the idea that Black children need to have confirmation of their intellectual capacity based on their history and cultural legacy. This is the essence of the Afrocentric idea.

Leaving the role of teacher in 1998, Wiggins founded her own charter school, Imhotep Institute Charter School, in Philadelphia, with an emphasis on technology and mathematics. She named the school "Imhotep" as a sign of respect for the first multidimensional genius in the African world, Imhotep, who built the first pyramid and established medicine as a science in the Nile Valley.

Numerous associations and organizations have recognized Wiggins for her brilliance and foundational knowledge about culturally relevant education. She has received awards from the National Council of Negro Women, the Cheikh Anta Diop International Conference, and the City of Philadelphia Mayor's Office.

Using the Seven Principles, the Nguzo Saba, and the concept of Maat as a foundation, Wiggins built her 600-student school on solid ideas from African culture. The Seven Principles have become a core part of any attempt to create revolutionary pedagogy. Established in the 1960s as keys to Kawaida philosophy as taught by the cultural philosopher Maulana Karenga, the Nguzo Saba became instruments for instruction and discipline in many schools. The principles in kiSwahili and English are as follows (Karenga, 1997):

1. *Umoja*, unity
2. *Kujichagulia*, self-determination
3. *Ujima*, collective work and responsibility
4. *Ujamaa*, cooperative economics
5. *Nia*, purpose
6. *Kuumba*, creativity
7. *Imani*, faith

Basing many of her instructive techniques on these principles, Mama Chris created an atmosphere that was structured, definitive, and disciplined. However, Wiggins's school ran into trouble with its board after 12 years of solid work. In effect, members of the board who did not understand Afrocentricity or the ideas behind passionate love and nurturing of students in a revolutionary manner sought to rein in the school's idealistic objectives. Ultimately, the founder of the school had to leave her creation, which had become an institution without the principles she had fought to ensure. Wiggins is a heroic figure, although the process and the project of the school was hindered due to the tragedy of misguided and inappropriate leadership. Revolutionary pedagogy is not without its challenges, both internal and external; but it is truly on the right side of history. Teachers have joined this movement even without support from the administration, but where they have the support of principals, they will continue to grow in number and to combat ignorance.

Priscilla Agbeo speaks about her experiences with revolutionary teachers at a Chicago school led by Lamailede Assata Moore. According to Agbeo (2016), when she needed the courage to lead, Moore gave her the opportunity to teach. Indeed, she writes that Moore made her feel like "I got this." Having been taught through modeling the ideas of self-identity and self-love, Abgeo demonstrated an intense emotional attachment to children's learning.

Also, the instructional counselor Shariba Rivers was the "epitome of divine Black womanhood for me," according to Agbeo (2016). She said that her "grace, intelligence, confidence, and overall energy moved me to carry myself like she did." There was something singularly important about the way Rivers carried herself as a teacher and counselor. This radiance that Agbeo sees in Rivers represents the kind of image that is ordinarily conveyed by those who love to teach.

CHAPTER 3

Situating a Revolutionary Pedagogy

Carter G. Woodson's (1933/2013) *The Mis-Education of the Negro* established the principles that influenced both the Afrocentric and the revolutionary pedagogy of this era. First published in 1933, Woodson's classic revealed the fundamental problem with the education of the African person in America to be the lack of knowledge of self. Since this is the first knowledge that is required to be sane and stable, the lack of it meant that African Americans were being educated against themselves. Indeed, as Woodson understood it, African Americans were educated to love the traditions and ideas of other people and cultures, and consequently, we were only attached to the fringes of European culture. Nah Dove (2021) brilliantly encapsulated Woodson's idea in this way:

> Woodson believed that being taught European-white (Eurocentric) economics, history, philosophy, religion and literature could only train the mind of the African-Black person to know her/his restricted place in society. In this way s/he will continue to support the power of the oppressor. It was clear that Woodson saw cultural distinctions between the experiences of European and African people and the negative impact of Eurocentric ideas on the African psyche. Woodson's idea was that to have "real" knowledge (Truth) would enable the liberation of the African mind and the destruction of false information. (p. 9)

Woodson (1933/2013) recognized that the African American student could not have a substantive and meaningful life within the context of

American society. Even during the nadir in race relations, Woodson did not reject American nationality or citizenship; he simply resolved to teach African Americans, who had not been long out of enslavement, how to shield against the most treacherous forms of cultural and social injustice. Woodson understood the peculiar relationship the African person had with the American nation, but he also knew that for the African to assume that he or she was in the same position as the European vis-à-vis the realities of America would mean spiritual, psychological, and cultural death.

Education for Woodson was at the top of the ladder for renewal and revolution. He saw that the elite class of educated Blacks had betrayed the community by running after European culture and ideas rather than recovering and reconstructing their own. He was disappointed with African American colleges because they were so deeply entrenched in the European ideology of white superiority that they simply became imitators of what had oppressed Africans.

Therefore, my principal impetus for the development of an Afrocentric response to the phenomenon of *dislocation* was Woodson's alert recognition, nearly 90 years ago, that there was something severely wrong with the way African Americans were being educated. Woodson could not understand why we could not be taught to appreciate and love our own culture first. It troubled him that the Black middle class had abandoned the love of African culture.

Afrocentricity seeks to respond to the dislocation of the African person by providing philosophical and theoretical guidelines and criteria that are centered in the person's perception of reality. A revolutionary pedagogy that would uplift students urges Native Americans, Mexican Americans, Asian Americans, and others who see their cultures underrepresented and misrepresented in the system of education to join the transformation of the system. Yet the African American community cannot and must not wait to begin the immediate implementation of the principles of a revolutionary pedagogy wherever we can. Our children are under severe stress and are psychologically harmed by the education they are receiving. In the 2014 book by Ama Mazama and Garvey Musumunu, *African Americans and Homeschooling*, the authors point out that most African Americans who home school their children do so because of the fear of racism in schools. This is not merely a fear of racist language against students but also a fear of racist attitudes and behaviors that model disdain for the incredible history of resistance and creativity in the Black world.

There can be nothing wrong with students viewing phenomena from the perspective of the African person. In education, this means that one provides students the opportunity to begin study of the world, its people, concepts, and history, from the point of view of the African child's heritage. Thus, the African American child is not an object but a subject, not someone who is only the descendant of enslaved persons but the descendant of those who resisted enslavement even to the end of their lives. No discipline of knowledge is alien to the African person from this perspective. Whether the subject is biology, medicine, literature, architecture, mathematics, or social studies, the African student is centered in the reality of that discipline so that he or she is not seen as "having to go get it" but rather as being a part of it. Peppered throughout the subject matter in the curriculum are the gems of inventive knowledge and intelligence.

Certainly, George Washington Carver, who occupies a central place in the emergence of America's agricultural revolution in the 20th century, must be seen as a model of brilliance and resolute determination to bring into existence an entire community of agrarian innovators. At Tuskegee Institute in Alabama, he dedicated his life to the laboratory in one of the great achievements of modern American education, planting seeds of genius throughout the world to the extent that the Soviet Union under Vladimir Lenin requested that he become the leader of their agricultural ministry. The fact of the matter is that he was not alone among African Americans in science. Indeed, he was no more than a descendant of Benjamin Banneker, who completed the work of L'Enfant in laying out the District of Colombia and giving the United States one of its first wooden clocks. I cite Carver and link him to Banneker as we should cite the continuity of this spirit of inventiveness in the African people. All revolutionary pedagogists must hunt down the strands of genius that can become fixtures in the way we think about any subject. There is nothing that has been achieved in any field that has not seen some African person engaged in it or something cognate to it. Although earlier African American historians, Africologists, and sociologists spent time in the redemptive mode of thinking that there had to be a Black person who can be isolated as a special genius to disprove white lies about the inferiority of Blacks, we now realize that those important responses made by intellectuals like John Hope Franklin, W. E. B. Du Bois, and Mary McLeod Bethune served the purpose of showing our innovative spirit although we were just up from enslavement. Contemporary Africans and Europeans know that the inferiority argument was bad bananas in the past and is even sillier among today's masses. In the past, we were quick to show that for every White scientist, scholar, and artist, there were equally talented Blacks. Hopefully, in an age when Kizzmenia Corbett, an African American woman, led the team that developed the Moderna vaccine against COVID-19, and Onyema Ogbuagu, a Nigerian man, was a principal researcher in the development of the Pfizer vaccine, we do not have to remind people that human intelligence is equally distributed among *Homo sapiens* population groups.

A revolutionary pedagogy is a quest for student centricity, and it encourages the locating of students within the context of their own cultural referent as a way of strengthening them in a multilayered universe where they are not on the periphery but share in the center of the thematic narrative. Thus, this applies to students from any culture. The most productive method of teaching a student is to place the student within the context of knowledge (Dei, 2010). For the White student in America, this goes without saying because almost all the experiences discussed in classes are from the standpoint of White history. This is as true for a discussion of the American Revolution as it is for a discussion of Dante's *Inferno*. Yet few students in high school have ever read a short story by John A. Williams, Alice Walker, or Paul Laurence Dunbar, three of the most gifted individuals ever to write in this country. What does this say about the absolute dismissal of Black cultural referents in the classroom? How does this play out in the lives of Black children? You can ask the same about the Vietnamese, Latinx, or Filipino student in the classroom.

I tend to believe that the vanguard people for changing America for the better have been the descendants of the enslavement because we came from such depths of depravity and experienced the most brutal of all evils in the society without being completely decimated, as happened to so many Native Americans. White enslavers both needed and hated Africans, and they rode the hard labor and deprivation of our people to their own wealth and power. The dominant society has a way of turning every event on its head so that schooling makes the victims the perpetrators of their own abuse; creates ideas of white generosity during white enmity toward a struggling people; and refuses to admit white guilt in the genocide of Native Americans and the enslavement of Africans. Thus, even a discussion of the European slave trade concentrates on what the whites were doing to Africans instead of the resistance of Africans. In such a world, the African student is always acted on but seldom shown to be an actor. A revolutionary pedagogy must be practiced in such a way that students from various cultures see themselves as participating in the flow of information and knowledge as well as in the resistance to all forms of human denials and negations.

Despite the powerful work that the eminent educator James A. Banks did in reasserting the five dimensions of multiculturalism, he faced resistance to this simple idea. Banks asked for five things: content integration, knowledge construction, equity pedagogy, prejudice reduction, and an empowering school culture (Banks, 2007; Banks & Banks, 2004). Revolutionary pedagogy incorporates all the dimensions of multiculturalism but adds a radical twist to the concept by insisting that white culture be seen as one of the cultures. It is not enough, for example, to speak of knowledge construction without giving some space for European-descended children in this process. After all, we all do construct knowledge, but what must be ensured is that white knowledge does not assume a position of superiority over that of other cultures. In the same vein, when Banks speaks of "equity pedagogy" and means by this term that teachers should adjust their teaching techniques to accommodate all cultures and genders, he is asserting a basic tenet of revolutionary pedagogy. The reason I have not simply adopted the term "equity pedagogy" is because revolutionary pedagogy demands much more than the teacher adopting a particular style; it demands that the teacher abandon certain ways of thinking about race and gender. Nevertheless, it is important to affirm the work done by Banks to redirect our thinking about multiculturalism because he recognized before most people the incredible beauty of diversity. I recall being invited to speak at the University of Washington in the late 1990s, where I laid out the tenets of Afrocentricity to an audience that included Banks, whose response found resonance with many of the ideas that I had articulated. I believe that this was largely because my work was based on transcending the race paradigm. In fact, my earliest works at the University of California at Los Angeles (UCLA) were on African American culture, transracial and interracial communication, and ultimately international communication. In a multicultural world, humanity is one, and the social constructions devised by European writers to separate the "races" were a misguided attempt to enforce a hierarchy that could not last.

In a multicultural nation, the best way to educate children is by using genuine multicultural perspectives based on equity for everyone, including whites. I have always seen multiculturalism as the quality of respecting and accepting a variety of cultural perspectives in education without hierarchy. The fact that European culture is the majority culture in the United States is no reason for it to be imposed as universal. Education, to have integrity, must begin with the proposition that all humans have contributed to the national discourse on transforming schools.

THREE PROPOSITIONS FOR REVOLUTIONARY PEDAGOGY

I suggest three propositions for a revolutionary pedagogy based on Afrocentric infusion:

1. Education is fundamentally a social phenomenon; it consists in socializing children. Of course, pedagogy is a political act in the sense that it allows the teacher to assume that he or she knows best what and how to teach.
2. To send a child to school is to prepare the child for being part of a social group. If the teacher assumes that the child cannot become a part of the preferred social group, then the child is often prepared for a different path and the discourse turns to what we can do with these children.

3. Societies develop schools that are suited to them. Hence, a White supremacist system develops white supremacist education.

The goal of the revolutionary pedagogist is to penetrate the curtain of ignorance with the sharpest analysis of the smothering fabric of defeat covering or hiding the genius of children. Let the children breathe in the air of African and African American cultural narratives, which all good educators have seen as positive weapons against anomie. In late 2016, Nigel Roberts wrote a powerful piece for *NewsOne* on what he called the "10 Unsung Heroes of Education." I was honored to be a part of the list, which included Fanny Jackson Coppin, Marva Collins, Edmund Gordon, William Leo Hansberry, Charles H. Houston, Kelly Miller, Frederick Douglas Patterson, Mary Jane Patterson, and Inez Beverly Prosser. When you examine the lives of the great educators, one thing that leaps out quickly is that they loved teaching Black students, and by extension, all students. They had a belief in the possibility of changing lives. They were obsessed with winning the student over and were willing to set up a contest between themselves and the student to make a difference. So one does not have to agree with all the ideological positions taken by these educators to see that they have been on the road to discovering greatness. Marva Collins started a school in her home in Chicago in 1975 because she knew that Black students could learn. Collins was neither an Afrocentrist nor a revolutionary pedagogist; she was a committed teacher who trained more than 1,000 teachers. When she set up Westside Preparatory School, a private elementary school in the impoverished Garfield Park section of Chicago, she wanted to prove that Black children could learn. One has to admire the tremendous spirit she demonstrated in making her school an example of what she thought was the best education for children.

Although I disagreed with her method, I understand full well what she was fighting against. Collins wanted to prove to naysayers that our children could master any of the histories, literatures, and science subjects that whites could master, so her program was steeped in classical European knowledge. What did she prove? She showed conclusively that Black children could learn anything that other children learn. However, I would have been more excited had she followed the pattern of Afrocentric educators like Barbara Sizemore, Wade Nobles, Freya Rivers, and Asa

Hilliard. Not only would the students have learned, as Rivers demon-strated, they would have excelled. Nevertheless, one cannot forget that Collins attempted to demonstrate that Black children were quite brilliant when it came to classroom learning. Yet part of the problem with con-temporary education is that so many people want our children to learn the ethics of a ruthless individualism that is totally out of touch with our African culture. We understand that the currency of our lives is relation-ships, and the relationships we have with each other and with our teachers, parents, and ancestors have to be at the center of our world.

We also have the testimonies about the clear insights and richly textured curriculum and resources originating with Maulana Karenga and Seba Limbiko Tembo, the leader of the African American Cultural Center's School in Los Angeles. Renamed after her as the Limbiko Tembo School for African American Culture, the school is an educational institute dedicated to inspiring children to reach for excellence. Accordingly, it stresses the responsibility of children to have a social consciousness, respect for human diversity, and a love of community service. Limbiko Tembo was teacher, vice principal and principal from 1979 to 2009. In a eulogy for her, Karenga (2009) wrote in the *Los Angeles Sentinel,*

> We know and honor you first as *Mwalimu,* teacher, speaker of the clear and mind-opening word, instructor in lessons of life and living, careful cultivator of the love for learning; rightfully attentive to the culture, the dignity and respect-demands of everyone; daring to give special rank and relevance even to an infant; Seba, moral teacher of the sacred word, tireless teacher of the good, the right and the possible and continuous student of the ancient teachings for insight, inspiration and ever-deeper understandings.

The special motto of Limbiko Tembo and others associated with the Limbiko Tembo School is "To do that which is of value is for eternity" (Karenga, 1984). Among the administrators and teachers of this school are Principal Mwalimu Thanayi Karenga, Vice Principal Mwalimu Thema Rikondja, Mwalimu Seba Chimbuko Tembo, Mwalimu Sanifu Adetona, Mwalimu Kojo Rikondja, and Mwalimu Hasani Soto. They are bound to teach the best values of African culture and make a concentrated effort to ensure that students recognize themselves as Africans with the right to be full participants of all knowledge. However, the first rule is to know who you are. The Limbiko Tembo School operates fundamentally as a Saturday school for children of ages 3–11 years. It focuses on African American history and culture.

One of the key educators to be passionate about the betrayal of Black boys was Jawanza Kunjufu, who took it on himself to study the rate at which schools sent Black boys to special education and then decided to write several important books on the subject. As early as 1985, Kunjufu wrote the first volume of *Countering the Conspiracy to Destroy Black Boys*. There were three more volumes and then he wrote the book *Keeping Black Boys Out of Special Education* (2005), an array of powerful indictments against a system that sought to blame everything that was wrong in the schools on the assertiveness of Black boys.

The escape hatch for African Americans must be the reorienting of the educational enterprise by raising the same questions that Woodson posed more than 50 years ago. One raises the questions as an assertive act by seeking in every situation the appropriate centrality of the African person (Asante, 1991). Thus, the persons of African descent should naturally be centered in their historical experiences as Africans. In education, this means that we do not marginalize children by placing them in positions that cause them to question their own self-worth because their story is seldom told. The little African American children who sit in a classroom and are made to accept as heroes and heroines individuals who defamed their people during their lifetime are being actively decentered, marginalized, and made nonpersons, whose aim in life might be to someday attempt to conceal their African origin and complexion as badges of inferiority rather than claim them as human traits of resilience and honor. Afrocentricity places these children in their proper historical setting.

Some African writers, professors, and artists rush to deny their "blackness" because they believe that to exist as a Black person is not to exist as a human being. These are the individuals who Woodson said preferred European art and languages to African art and languages, who believed that what was of European origin was inherently better than what their own people had produced. Eurocentric curricula produce such aberrations in the African person. A truly educated person would view both African and European education as significant and useful; indeed, a

White person who is educated in such a system would no longer assume superiority based on a false education.

THE REVOLUTIONARY CHALLENGE

The most revolutionary challenge to the ideology of White supremacy in education during the past decade was the Afrocentric idea. No other theoretical position stated by African Americans has ever captured the imagination of such a wide range of scholars and students of history, sociology, communication, anthropology, and psychology.

Three Critical Challenges to White Supremacist Teachings

Afrocentricity poses a revolutionary challenge to White supremacist education in three critical ways as discussed below:

1. It questions the imposition of the White supremacist view as universal history (classical, continental, explorers, etc.; Asante, 1990).
2. It assaults ignorance by demonstrating the indefensibility of the supporting racist theories about multiculturalism.
3. It radically projects a humanistic and pluralistic viewpoint (revolutionary pedagogy) by articulating Afrocentricity as a valid, nonhegemonic perspective in this regard while encouraging other cultures to do the same, so that Europe is not above others but seen properly within its own context.

Afrocentricity relates to revolutionary pedagogy as an essential step on the ladder to operationalizing the concept. Inasmuch as revolutionary pedagogy is about deconstructing and disrupting the status quo no, other philosophical paradigm has adequately started that process. Afrocentric education centers the child in history and culture rather than outside of it. It is therefore on the road to the paradigmatic state that is revolutionary. How alien must an African American child feel in those cases where the information being presented makes the child feel like an outsider? In most classrooms, whites are located in the center perspective position. Whatever the subject, the African person is on the outside. Nevertheless, as Collins has demonstrated, the

Black child, with the assistance of dedicated and committed teachers who believe in children, can master that information regardless of its dislocating effect. Even if we wanted a truly multicultural education, that also must initially be based on an Afrocentric perspective, otherwise the African American child will continue to be lost in the European framework. While all children can learn, the most valuable role the teacher can play, that is, the most ethical, is to begin with self-identity.

AFROCENTRICITY AND HISTORY

A few years before his death, Arthur Schlesinger and others formed what they called a "Committee for the Defense of History." But history needs no defense; only lies, untruths, and inaccurate information need defending. This committee was nothing more than an attempt to buttress the crumbling pillars of a White supremacist system that has maintained its legitimacy by concealing its motives behind the cloak of American neo-liberalism. Such a movement is in the same spirit and tradition as Allan Bloom's *The Closing of the American Mind* (2012) and E. D. Hirsch's *Cultural Literacy* (1988); both books were placed in the service of the white hegemony in education, particularly in curriculum, and Hirsch made millions of dollars when his work was considered by conservative politicians as useful for the Common Core in public schools.

Cheikh Anta Diop, the late great scholar, told me in Dakar, Senegal, in December, 1980, "African history and Africa need no defense." Thus, when I heard that there were White scholars, joined by some Blacks, who thought it was necessary to defend history, I knew that they must have had a lot of shoring up to perform. But perhaps in a discussion of the curriculum that would open it up in a profound way, it was inevitable that the closets of bigotry would reveal various attempts to defend White privilege in the curriculum as it had often been defended in the society. This was a predictable challenge to the thrust for pluralism. Their attempt was no more than a defense of the received interpretations of a racist history, written preeminently from a hegemonic, White supremacist perspective. Those who argue against the Africa-centered or Afrocentric perspective often clothe their arguments in false categories and fake terms (Keto, 1991).

Afrocentric education is not *against* history: it is *for* history, correct, accurate history. If it is against anything, it is against marginalizing African American, Latin American, Asian American, and Native American children—a true revolutionary pedagogy will be different from a racist education, that is, a White supremacist education.

Frankly, perhaps the most unsettling aspect of revolutionary pedagogy for many whites and some African Americans is that its narrative power and its analytical power are derived from Afrocentric authors. Of course, as we know, some white writers and many Asians have written outside the Western box. I am thinking particularly of the works by C. K. Raju (2009) and Ana Monteiro Ferreira (2015). Raju's push to decolonize the universities around the world and Ferreira's critique of modernism and postmodernism may represent aspects of this new revolutionary pedagogy. White Americans and Europeans have always had charge of the major ideas in the American academy. Deconstruction, Gestalt psychology, Marxism, structuralism, early-childhood education, and so on, have been articulated, elaborated on, and developed by White scholars. On the other hand, Afrocentricity is the product of mainly African and African American scholars, such as Ama Mazama, Wade Nobles, Asa Hilliard, Maulana Karenga, and C. T. Keto. On the African continent, the works of Simphiwe Sesanti and Vusi Gumede offer new insights into the discourse around revolutionary pedagogy. Indeed, there are increasing numbers of young African American scholars and some young White scholars influenced by philosophers like Frantz Fanon and Lewis Gordon, who have begun to write in the revolutionary vein.

Fanon is a patron saint of confrontation of negativity, and hence he exists as someone who could profoundly teach us how to approach pedagogy in a world of conflicts. In discussing the complexity of the colonial situation in Algeria, Fanon (Fanon, 1961/2005) wrote directly of the need for confronting violence.

> You do not turn any society, however primitive it may be, upside down with such a program if you have not decided from the very beginning, that is to say from the actual formulation of that program, to overcome all the obstacles that you will come across in so doing. The native who decides to put the program into practice, and to become its moving force, is ready

for violence at all times. From birth it is clear to him that this narrow world, strewn with prohibitions, can only be called in question by absolute violence. (p. 37)

Of course, Fanon was speaking in the context of a war for independence in the colonized nation of Algeria. For us, the lesson is less absolute, but nevertheless, we must be ready to confront paranoid fantasies that seek to dominate our thinking.

To understand fully the essence of Fanon's philosophy of education, it is necessary to have an idea of the world in which he lived. Without a proper location of his place in the world, we are unaware of the motives that generate a statement like "I came into the world imbued with the will to find a meaning in things, my spirit filled with the desire to attain to the source of the world, and then I found that I was an object in the midst of other objects" (Fanon, 1952/1967, p. 109). Here, Fanon is expressing himself, as so many other Blacks have expressed themselves, in the throes of self-discovery while sitting in a classroom listening to the report of yet another white intellectual. Fanon was conscious of the white gaze, what every Black child in a classroom with a majority of White students must feel, the hegemonic thinking of White individuals or teachers who pictured him and others like him as objects on the periphery of humanity and knowledge. This observation was a part of his salvation, if indeed we can ever say that Fanon saw clearly enough to be saved. "Mama, the nigger is going to eat me up," Fanon (1952/1967) has the little White boy crying to his mother in "The Fact of Blackness" (*Black Skin, White Masks*, chap. 5). In this facet of his understanding, Fanon knows that he is the subject, although he is quick to say that he is an object among other objects; but alas, this is the case only in hegemonic societies where whites see blacks only as objects, whether in schools or outside schools. Fanon is located in the engine of agency; he reacts not like an object but like one fully in control of his will.

The idea of agency has two important parts: (1) the spirited will to save oneself and others and (2) acceptance of the critical responsibility that comes with agency. The first part is almost automatic once a person gains consciousness of the historical crime that has been committed against Africans and other systematically oppressed people. It is almost a reaction in the interest of personal safety and security. It is as if the person says, "I cannot allow the oppressor to stand in the way of my will; if necessary, I *will* do everything in my power to eliminate oppression even if it means being violent against the oppressor." In schools, this is the student who *refuses* to learn or *refuses* to engage in the classroom as an act of resistance.

I call this a spirited will because it is not simply knowledge or consciousness but an active participation in one's freedom. It is the spirit that is manifested in Nat Turner, Harriet Tubman, and Fannie Lou Hamer. The second part of agency carries a very high ethical responsibility; that is what I mean when I call it a critical responsibility. Fanon understood that we are the authors of our destiny but that each human being has to make a series of decisive breaks in order to be truly human. When I am able to see clearly enough with the consciousness that I have gained, I will be able to understand that it is only when I have centered myself in my own historical and existential reality that I will be able to make a proper moral judgment of myself and my fellows. If, in my mind, I am in the margins of human history or on the fringes of historical reality, I will never be able to think of myself as properly human, meaning properly responsible, and hence I will forever be a victim. Of course, I cannot be held accountable for my actions either, because I am an object, one that might be fabricated as a commodity and sold on television or the web as a black body. In education, I become a number, a test score, or a statistic but never the subject of my own narrative, and those who read me or listen to me only do so out of a sense of superiority to me. I am therefore nothing more than a commodity in the classroom. How much money can the school get from the federal government?

In many ways, Fanon speaks clearly and profoundly to me personally because I have refused to surrender my rage, a significantly human part of me, in the face of patriarchy, prejudice, homophobia, sexism, White privilege, and capitalist greed. Since I have never seen myself as, nor do I seek to become, a *public intellectual*, I cannot be seduced by material trinkets. As an *activist intellectual*, however, I intend to pursue to the greatest extent possible the overthrow of all forms of academic tyranny and intellectual terror against Black students. As an African, I see this intention as part of my challenge to enthrone a kingdom of *Maat* with its attendant ideas of justice, righteousness, harmony, balance, truth, order, and reciprocity. What this really means to me, a revolutionary pedagogist, is that we must work to bring into existence a world that Fanon would have sought.

The world made by Fanon is one quite familiar by now to revolutionary pedagogists who seek to establish rationality at the center of the academic being. What can be greater for a person than to be seen as a participant in the drama of life rather than a spectator to dramas being played out by others? To be inside the drama, acting and performing with intelligence and rationality, is to be at the center of the cosmos, as far as we know the cosmos. I mean we do not know everything, and that was even obvious to the brilliant Fanon, but we know enough to believe that those who have been pushed off of their own terms, alienated as it were from their own histories, names, values, and traditions cannot act rationally without being recentered. To liberate one's self is both to break through to agency and to refuse to allow others, whatever their status, to violate you. For me, it is this realization at the moment of decision that marks the most powerful identification of personal and collective liberation with genuine education.

Domination of others is a type of colonialism, even if on a personal scale; resistance to domination is a type of anticolonialism. Like Fanon, the revolutionary pedagogist sees domination, whether physical or linguistic or in any other form, as a challenge for a regimen of resistance. Nothing should ever force us to allow the codification of domination or any other Western modernist notion of controlling space and place to subvert our liberation. In effect, you must be ready to fight against all types of conformist rhetoric, action, or education.

Suppression and Distortion

African American scholars trained in the best universities and with some of the most impressive credentials have now emerged with ideas about how to change the curriculum Afrocentrically. The forces of resistance to this transformation began to assemble around their wagons almost as quickly as the word was given that education had to treat each child equally. The attempt was to discredit the intellectual and philosophical movement because White scholars at the major universities did not start it and have not discovered how to articulate it. Yet even without the ability to quote a single word on the theory, they write articles against Afrocentricity, often criticizing it as a separatist movement, a further indication of their lack of knowledge. This is another example of arrogant Eurocentrism, which assumes that unless whites originated the idea it is unworthy of serious consideration. Have we ever called an idea that emerged out of the mind of a white thinker separatist simply because it came from a White person? The Black students who study in the classrooms of some of these teachers and professors know more about the term "Afrocentricity" than their professors because they have read the books. The idea that an African American child learns from a stronger position if she is centered, that is, sees herself *in* the story rather than from the margins, is not novel (Asante, 2003), but it is revolutionary when we begin to teach teachers how to put the child in the story.

THE CONDITIONS OF EDUCATION

The institutions in a society reflect the character of the society. Crime, education, and politics are different in different nations because of their societies. In the United States, we have practiced a whites-only orientation in education. This has had a profound impact on the quality of education for all children. The African American child has suffered out of proportion to White children, who also are victims of diseased curricula. One value of Afrocentric education is that it teaches discipline, that is, it empowers the teacher because discipline is based on the quality of ethical authority that comes from truth. Children submit to discipline to show devotion to a group for which they have respect.

THE TRANSFORMATION OF PERSPECTIVE

Afrocentric education represents a new interpretation of the productive transmission of values and attitudes. Students are made to see with new eyes and to hear with new ears. African American children learn to interpret phenomena from their position as centered; whites learn to see that their own centers are not threatened by the space taken by African Americans or others. Using the strong legs of Afrocentricity, a revolutionary pedagogist can reshape the thinking of children about learning. In some senses, what the revolutionary pedagogist does is what the African American teachers did during the gloomiest period of segregation; they subverted the system, and when they were given second-hand books to bring to the Black children sitting in the classroom, those teachers, without ever naming themselves, became the agents of transformation and made thousands of young Black children feel that they could do anything because, despite what the texts said or did not say, Africans had built the pyramids and the stone cities of Zimbabwe.

Revolutionary pedagogy works for all children because it is correct and accurate. Now here is the thing: Most White Americans are ignorant about African American history or culture, yet African Americans study and debate white history and culture. Our Black students have vast experiences with the white world, but the white world, at least in America, knows next to nothing about Black people. Very few White professors have ever had a course in African American studies and therefore are unable to provide systematic information about African Americans. Unfortunately, much the same is true of Black professors, who have usually been taught by White professors.

We are victims of the same system. Our children do not know the names of the African ethnic groups that constitute our population; we do not know the names of any sacred sites in Africa; we can hardly tell you what the Middle Passage was and meant to Africans; and we have forgotten the brutality of slavery and celebration of freedom.

THE TRAGEDY OF IGNORANCE OF OUR OWN HISTORY

Our children have little understanding of the nature of the private and state capture, the transport, and the enslavement of Africans. How many of us were truly taught the horrors of being taken and shipped naked across 25 days of ocean, seeing others leap singing to their deaths, being broken by abuse and indignities of all kind, and then being dehumanized to a thing without a name? If we knew, perhaps our behavior would be different. If our children had to read the slave narratives and the ship captain's words, they would be different, the White children would be different, and America would be a different nation.

They should have heard the story of how the barbaric treatment began, how the African's dignity was stolen, and how culture was destroyed. They should have known the story of how death swam next to the ships in the dreaded Middle Passage. A few Africans recorded their experiences: Jacob and Ruth Weldon, an African couple, gave the most detailed account ever found (Feldstein, 1971).

They wrote that the African, having been captured and brought onto the ships,

> was chained on the deck, made to bend over, and branded with a red hot iron in the form of letters or signs dipped in an oily preparation and pressed against the naked flesh till it burnt a deep and ineffaceable scar, to show who was the owner. (Feldstein, 1971, p 35)

The Weldons said that "those who screamed were lashed in the face, breast, thighs, and backs with cat-o-nine tails wielded by White sailors. Every blow brought the returning lash pieces of grieving flesh" (Feldstein, 1971, pp. 33–37). The Weldons continued that they saw "mothers with babies at their breasts basely branded and lashed, hewed and scarred, till it would seem as if the very heavens must smite the infernal tormentors with the doom they so richly merited" (Feldstein, 1971, p. 36).

If only the children of America could read the words of the Weldons:

> The male slaves were chained two by two, at the arm and leg. Women were stowed away without chains but naked, and all were packed away in the holes of ships for the five to eight week trip across the sea. The Africans could not even sit upright, the space between the decks being only two feet in height. On fair weather days the Africans were allowed to come on deck and dance for exercise. This they did with leg irons and chains to prevent them from escaping. Even some of the slave ship captains said the "groans and suffocating cries for air and water coming from below the deck sickened the soul of humanity." (Feldstein, 1971, p. 36)

Compelled to wiggle for space and to moan the long hours of night away in horror, with no fresh water to quench the tormenting thirst in a tightly squeezed space on the ship, with just enough oxygen to prolong their claustrophobic suffering, our ancestors vowed in those dark, damp, dank hell holes of horror that we would be free one day. Our children do not know the story. And White children do not know the story. If they were taught the revolutionary pedagogy perspective on the Great Enslavement, they would be different. Remembrance is necessary for humility and understanding. This is why the Jewish community has rightly campaigned to get the European Holocaust taught in schools and colleges across the world. Such a monstrous human brutality should remind the world of how humans have often violated one another. Teaching about the African Holocaust is just as important for some of the same reasons; essentially, it underscores the enormity of the dislocation of Africans, physically, psychologically, and economically. Without understanding the historical experiences of Africans, one cannot truly make any headway in dealing with the problems of the present.

There are those who will say that education should begin with the arrival of Africans in the English colonies because that is where African American history begins. That would be a mistake for several reasons. In the first place, 1619 was not the first time that Africans were in the Americas. Furthermore, on the slave ships, it is true that the weak perished and the strong stayed alive, meaning essentially that America became something of a home for those who survived. Yet the experience on the ships created an entirely different history for Africans from that of whites, who came on their own and most often not against their will. The Africans' sleeping and resting places were often covered with blood and mucous, and the horrid stench of the dead, breeding yet others for death, was everywhere. Those who survived often looked on the dead beside them and intoned, "Gone to she own country" or "Gone to he own friends."

Instructional Testimonies

The slave captains did not spare even infants and children from the terror. The Weldons tell of a child of nine months being flogged because he would not eat. This failing, the captain ordered the child's feet placed in boiling water, which dissolved the skin and nails, and then the child was whipped again. Still refusing to eat, the child had a piece of mango wood tied to his neck as punishment. When nothing would make this baby eat, the captain took him and slammed him from his arms onto the deck. The child died instantly. The mother was called and asked to throw the dead body overboard. She refused and was beaten. Then she was forced to take the corpse of her baby to the ship's side, where "with her head averted so she might not see it, she dropped the body into the sea" (Feldstein, 1971, p. 37).

If our children knew the African American's struggle, as they ought to know, they would find a renewed sense of purpose and vision. If White children knew this, rather than the pablum of deceit that is normally given to them about the European slave trade, they would rise up and not only see differently but also work to create a better place. If our children knew that the captain of a ship with 440 Africans on board had 132 thrown overboard in order to save water, they would cease acting as if they have no past or no reason to live.

When those slave ships reached land, whatever the land, whatever the condition, the Africans thought that nothing could be as bad as the Middle Passage, with its long bloody night of violence and terror. Here, on land, however, the situation was often worse. Mothers were often forced to leave their children alone in the slave shacks while they worked in the fields. Unable to nurse these children or to care for them, they often returned from work at night to find their children dead (Feldstein, 1971).

If our children could really read history and see the relationship of Africans to cotton, women, and children working till

> the blood runs from the tips of their fingers, where they have been pricked by the hard pod; or if they could see them dragging their baskets, all trembling, to the scale, for fear their weight should be short, and they should get the flogging which in such a case they know they must expect; or if they could see them bent double with constant stooping, and scourged on their bare back when they attempted to rise to straighten themselves for a moment, (Feldstein, 1971, p. 49)

they would treat each cotton shirt or dress as a sacred fabric, just as our brothers and sisters in the Caribbean and in Colombia and Brazil treat sugar with reverence because of the pain it had caused our African people.

If they had only heard the testimony of Henry Bibb (1850), who said,

> I was born May 1815, of a slave mother . . . and was claimed as the prop-
> erty of David White, Esq. . . . I was flogged up; for where I should have
> received moral, mental, and religious instructions, I received stripes with-
> out number, the object of which was to degrade and keep me in
> subordination. I can truly say, that I drank deeply of the bitter cup of
> suffering and woe. I have been dragged down to the lowest depths of
> human degradation and wretchedness, by slaveholders. (p. 1)

Correcting Distorted Information

Hegemonic education can only exist so long as true and accurate information is kept from the people. With information, people will have new
inputs into the reasons for whether they want to follow these paths or
not. You can no longer be comfortable with teaching that Greece is the
home of philosophy if you realize that the Greeks taught that Africa,
specifically Kemet, was the home of the origin of philosophy. You cannot
teach the European origin of art if you know about the Black people of
ancient Kemet. Hegemonic education can exist only so long as whites
think that Africans have never contributed to civilization. It is largely
based on such false ideas that invidious distinctions are made.

AFRICAN PHILOSOPHERS

Not only did Africa contribute to human history, but African civilizations
predate any that we know about since humans originated on the continent of
Africa. This is true whether you take archaeological evidence or biological
evidence into account. Let us leave Greece and the Greeks and return to study
Egypt and the Egyptians. Let us study the first philosophers: Kagemni, Khun-
anup, Ptahhotep, Kete, Duauf, Akhenatonn, Amenomope, Amenemhat, and
Seti. But since our education about ourselves is so disjointed, we have no way
of seeing an organic relationship between Africa and the rest of human history. With our enslavement came an attack on our psychical and spiritual
being. The ontological onslaught caused some Africans to opt for suicide.
Enslavement was a living death; the brutality of the slavocracy is unequalled
for its psychological destruction of African Americans. This gave us a freedom

faith. However, the results were often *dislocation, disorientation,* and *misori-entation*—all conditions of being decentered. The African in this situation is one who has "shed" or tried to shed race, to become raceless. One's basic identity is self-identity, which is ultimately one's cultural identity. Without a cultural identity, you are lost. You can no more divest yourself of your race or your culture than you can stop breathing oxygen and still live. We are African and human; others are European and human. There is no contradiction in either position. Humans come in many types, colors, and cultures. So we have to sing with our ancestors, "Wade in the waters, children, don't you get weary."

We have been mesmerized, tranquilized, and paralyzed when it comes to the education of African American children. Generations before us who came out of the enslavement and became the fastest group of illiterates to ever achieve literacy and who built schools in their churches and taught their families to read and write when only one or two of the family members had any knowledge of English inspire us to construct an authentic response to schools. But we must face up to the challenges that confront pupils each day and defy the negative predictions of the impossible. We know that our history is full of victories over those who have underestimated our ability to succeed. How is it that our ancestors were able to build colleges with pennies and then dared to call them universities, and some teachers and administrators want to say that African American children cannot be motivated? It is often not a motivational problem but a content issue, what is being taught and how.

SYMBOLS OF RESISTANCE

There is the idea that there are two discourses about multiculturalism. Different adherents to the theory have different views on what it means. There is only one discourse that is relevant to the liberation of the minds of African and White people in the United States, and that one is based on acceptance of Africa as central to African people in terms of *place, location, foundation,* and *history* as the starting point for any discussion. Diane Ravitch (1990) argues that there is a *pluralist multiculturalism* and a *particularist multiculturalism.* I have said this is nonsense because it confuses the fundamental problem we confront in a racist society. These

ideas exist only in Ravitch's imagination. Either you are for multiculturalism or you are not. The divisions she advances are really to conceal her
position. We can say that a person either supports the maintenance of
White supremacist teachings and constructions in education or does not;
there is no other possibility. Support of these positions depends on keeping other people ignorant. Information must be distorted or suppressed,
books never written or, if written, never published, or, if published,
banned from the school district. All of these tactics are the tactics of those
who prefer Africans to remain on the mental and psychological plantation. Ravitch was called the leader of the professors who opposed
multiculturalism in the 1990s. But since their positions are indefensible
on that score, they argue that they are for multiculturalism, which
means—when you read their works—that they are for *a white perspective on everybody else's culture.* I call these professors resisters because
they are attempting to resist the progressive transformation of a mono-
ethnic curriculum. The resisters say that Afrocentricity is antiwhite. If
Afrocentricity as a theory is against anything, it is against racism, ignorance, and white hegemony in curriculum. This is not antiwhite; it is
prohuman. Others have written that it brings about the *tribalization* of
America, but America already has red state and blue state divisions, with
a large clan of whites who voted for former president Donald Trump, for
example, because they saw in him a leader of a tribe that felt threatened
and under severe stress because of the increasing multicultural nature of
the society. I believe that revolutionary pedagogy provides all Americans
an opportunity to accept and promote a more equitable understanding
of the nation. This is important because the transmission of common
values should be at the center of education. This can only happen if we
see that the African person, since the beginning of the nation, has moved
from the periphery of the narrative to a place where we all share in the
center. No one raises an eyebrow at Chinatowns in America, and no one
should; yet when African people seek to create from their historical and
cultural center, they are often met with a negative reaction. Is this reaction really about who should be permitted to be on or off the plantation?

Pluralism is recognition of our difference. America is already divided if
you speak of opportunities afforded in education to children. The White
child by virtue of the protection provided by the society and enforced by

the curriculum is already ahead of the African American child in first grade. We have got to focus on giving the African American child opportunities at the prekindergarten level. But the kind of assistance the child needs is as much cultural as academic and must be in tandem with giving the White child the kind of support necessary to diminish the idea of privilege. Indeed, if the cultural information is provided, the academic transformation will follow. The aim of the Afrocentric curriculum and revolutionary pedagogy is not to divide America but to make America flourish as it ought to.

Some resisters claim that history is being created simply because they do not know the facts. No one has ever proved that history was being created. Can you imagine how arrogant it is for someone to speak of "fantasy history" and "bizarre theories" when they have never read the facts or heard the arguments? What they have highlighted is the fact that they did not know something. But it is very arrogant to claim that something is created just because you have never heard of it. The only reigning initiative of the total change proposed and led by Africans is the movement to transform curriculum and introduce a new revolutionary pedagogy. Instead of getting on board to fight against white hegemonic education, some whites and some Blacks too have decided to plead for a return to the education plantation. However, those days are gone and can never be packaged as accurate, correct education again.

MYTHS ABOUT EDUCATION

We know that our children have been maligned. Our history has been maligned. Our continent of origin has been maligned. We also know that our teachers have often been maligned. But let me give you two truisms about education in America. First, *some teachers can and do teach African American children effectively.* Second, *if they can do it, then we can learn what their attitudes are about teaching that makes them successful.* Among the myths we often hear about schools and education are the following.

1. *African American children have the same advantages as whites. In which school district does this happen?*

America has become a nation of criminals, discriminators, and educators who kill little children's motivation. At no point in American history has it been the case that African American children have had the same advantages as whites. You would have to close your eyes to reality in order to make a statement supporting the equality of opportunity. There is not a predominantly African American school in any district in America that is considered the equivalent of a predominantly white school in the same district. I am not talking about the brightness of the students; I am talking about the treatment of students and the expenditures on the schools. The experiences of African Americans are not the same. No other group of people has had such a long campaign against its history and culture. The aim has been to wipe out African identity. There are several myths that add to the misinformation about education. Those who provide information are often operating on the basis of these false myths.

2. *The treatment of African American children is the same as that of White children. In which school is this really the case?*

If you believe this myth, then you are ready to be sold the George Washington Bridge. Whether you speak of the historical relationship to the school environment, textbook publishers, boards of education, or teachers' responses to students, our children are not treated equally. I am not saying, treated *the same*; I am saying, treated *equally*.

Most of all, the context for learning is different—the names of buildings, models for learning experiences, trips to places of cultural value to the students, and invitations to writers and speakers.

3. *There is ample information about Africans in the curriculum. Why would someone make such an ignorant statement when the entire curriculum is about White people and their deeds and misdeeds?*

School curricula see Africans as guests; consequently, there is little modeling of events and personalities. White students may ask the teacher who teaches about Africans, "Is it going to be on the test?" If not, then they often do not consider the information as an organic part of the subject under discussion. Why should little African children have to see themselves as guests when their ancestors are interwoven with the building of the nation?

STRATEGIES FOR IMPLEMENTATION

There are several steps necessary for implementing a revolutionary peda-gogy and an Afrocentric curriculum for change. Indeed, attention to the language in the scope and sequence of the curriculum is one of the easiest ways to assess the situation in a school curriculum. What type of words and terms are used to refer to African peoples? Are these words pejora-tives? Can they be changed to reflect the realities of the situation? Among the steps to be considered are the following points for discussion:

1. *Language issues:* Pay attention to terms such as "slavery," "bush-man," "pygmies," "minority," "co-culture," "subcultures," "Black Africa," and "tribe" and phrases like "a bunch of wild Indians."
2. Strong involvement of teachers, parents, and churches is needed after school.
3. Understand the ideas of *scope, sequence,* and *objectives* as they relate to curriculum.
4. De-bias attitudes as well as facts by looking for assertions that are biased in the way they are stated.

Radical Introduction of African Content

Afrocentric education is a radical introduction of African content into the curriculum to change the quality of the educational experience for African American students and to create enough factual bases for a new understanding of knowledge by other students. However, it is not mere contributionism that is the center of Afrocentric education but integrated and infused information. Afrocentric education is therefore a fundamen-tal necessity for anyone declaring competence in almost any subject in America; otherwise, the person remains essentially ignorant of a major portion of the world. Thus, Afrocentric infusion is a core element of revolutionary pedagogy.

Furthermore, multiculturalism, to be authentic, must consider the Afrocentric perspective, which is the proper stepping stone from the African American culture to a true multiculturalism. If this step is skipped, we are likely to see an idea of multiculturalism that is defined through the eyes of whites, without any substantive African American information infused into the curriculum. I think we are fairly clear that as we march toward revolutionary pedagogy, we can skip neither an Afrocentric curriculum nor proper multiculturalism. They are incorporated into the new orientation to education.

CHAPTER 4

The Principles of the Pedagogy of Revolution

I arrived at revolutionary pedagogy from my position as a descendant of enslaved Africans, knowing fully well that all education originates from the intentions, obligations, desires, and ambitions that one finds in societies. To change the nature of pedagogy and the content of curriculum means that we must also change the nature of society's objectives for educating people. This is the revolution that must happen to ensure the effective and useful education of children.

This book deals with the politics of education and analyzes how we must overturn the oppressive conditions of education and create a revolutionary pedagogy. My objective is to make it possible for the teacher to challenge all forms of racist knowledge and to assert through a powerful pedagogical ethic a new vision of education.

I do not think that teachers generally express racist views. I do not believe that administrators of schools think that they are supporting racism. Yet in most instances they are doing nothing to challenge the oppressive symbols, images, ideas, concepts, content, and pedagogy that exist in their schools. The truth of the matter is that without a conscious reading and thinking about teaching you will undoubtedly create or re-create racial pedagogy.

REVOLUTIONARY PEDAGOGY AND
NECESSARY OBJECTIVES

Here is what a revolutionary pedagogy must do:

It must challenge the educational vision perpetrated by the oppressive system of racism.

It must defend students from the self-hatred that invades their spirits.

It must play a role in supporting agency for those who have been marginalized by the system of education in terms of concepts, themes, and curricular ideas.

It must demonstrate methods for combating agency reduction in the academy

It must counteract and contradict negations of African agency and narratives.

Any idea that education is neutral is nothing more than political posturing. All education is political and has lifestyle and policy implications. In a revolutionary pedagogy, we seek to expose all the myths of educational neutrality promoted by those who control the reins of power. In effect, a revolutionary pedagogy is subversive to the oppressive curriculum that is meant to mold the minds of children to be consumers, clients, and victims. In this respect, revolutionary pedagogy opposes the sexist and racist indoctrination that is often a serious component of the curricula of American education. I do not mean that this occurs in an overt manner, because most of the time it is a covert racism and sexism, something that is not expressed but is practiced and lived.

One of the challenges of revolutionary pedagogy is to change the status quo with regard to hiding behind the idea of universalism. Whether this is the assertion that science has a universal character or that what is considered classical is universal, the idea is false and consequently at the core of what must be overturned. Those who say, "Get politics out of schools" are the very ones who are maintaining politics in schools. It is disconcerting that those who attack racism and sexism in the curriculum are considered subversive while those who use the curriculum to represent the status quo are considered mainstream.

How revolutionary pedagogy can be applied to change the focus of education so that students benefit is the subject of this project. We all know that racism or racial hegemony is not merely a physical issue but an issue of ideas, art, and practice. Thus, the abstract becomes real, the symbolic is presented in the act of teaching, and pedagogy comes alive because of the teacher.

Carter G. Woodson, Mary McLeod Bethune, Asa Hilliard, Barbara Sizemore, Jawanza Kunjufu, and Joyce King have been some of the boldest champions of transformative education in the history of America. Woodson (1933/2013) wrote in the *Mis-Education of the Negro* that the African American was not properly educated because he was educated away from himself, from his history, from his own narratives.

> If you can control a man's thinking you do not have to worry about his action. When you determine what a man shall think you do not have to concern yourself about what he will do. If you make a man feel that he is inferior, you do not have to compel him to accept an inferior status, for he will seek it himself. If you make a man think that he is justly an outcast, you do not have to order him to the back door. He will go without being told; and if there is no back door, his very nature will demand one. (p. 21)

Woodson was a revolutionary in the sense that he wanted African Americans to study their own history and culture as a base for following other forms and avenues of education. He was well aware that it was not in the interest of whites to properly educate Blacks; this had to be something that Blacks would take up. Thus, Woodson (1933/2013) wrote,

> Philosophers have long conceded, however, that every man has two educators: that which is given to him, and the other that which he gives himself. Of the two kinds of education, the latter is by far the more desirable. Indeed, all that is most worthy in man he must work out and conquer for himself. It is that which constitutes our real and best nourishment. What we are merely taught seldom nourishes the mind like that which we teach ourselves. (p. 15)

In my judgment, it is impossible to move children to the point of wanting to study or acquire knowledge if they do not have a truly radical reading of history. All scholars who have studied the nature of information have concluded that oppressors will never teach the oppressed how to break their chains; this they must do for one another. It was Woodson who anticipated revolutionary pedagogy, and I have always paid respect to him ("The Afrocentric Idea in Education," Asante, 1991). I was further encouraged by Woodson's strong belief that we had learned the music and culture of everyone but the African's. Woodson (1933/2013) said that "to handicap a student by teaching him that his black face is a curse and that his struggle to change his condition is hopeless is the worst sort of lynching" (p. 22). I think today he would add that to teach children by commission or omission that their ancestors never created civilizations, culture, inventive tools, or arts is also a form of lynching, mental lynching.

Mary McLeod Bethune called for Africans to proclaim their heroes, monuments, and personalities in order to demonstrate the strength and brilliance of the African people. In her famous speech "Clarifying Our Vision With the Facts," delivered on October 31, 1937, before the Association for the Study of Negro Life and History (published in 1938 in *The Journal of Negro History*), Bethune said of Black children,

> When they learn of the fairy tales of mythical king and queen and princess, we must let them hear, too, of the pharaohs and African kings and brilliant pageantry of the Nile Valley; when they learn of Caesar and his legions we must teach them of Hannibal and his Africans; when they learn of Shakespeare and Goethe we must teach them of Pushkin and Dumas. (pp. 11–12)

So powerful were Bethune's remembrances of the glorious history of African people—founded on the same philosophy that she had used to bring into existence her organization National Council of Negro Women two years earlier in 1935—that high leaders of the nation, including First Lady Eleanor Roosevelt, were influenced by her. In many ways, Bethune and Woodson were on the same wavelength. Woodson (1933/2013) said,

> If you teach the Negro that he has accomplished as much good as any other race he will aspire to equality and justice without regard to race. Such an effort would upset the program of the oppressor in Africa and America. Play up before the Negro, then, his crimes and shortcomings. Let him learn to admire the Hebrew, the Greek, the Latin and the Teuton. Lead the Negro to detest the man of African blood—to hate himself.(p. 16)

Bethune and Woodson knew that the best educator was the one who offered love of the children as a central revolutionary idea. As a master teacher himself and a brilliant trainer of teachers, Asa Hilliard (n.d.) would often say,

> I have never encountered any children in any group who were not geniuses. There is no mystery on how to teach them. The first thing you do is to treat them like human beings and the second thing is to love them.

And he knew that when you begin to do things that will raise the achievement levels of the poorest and disenfranchised students "you may not get applause." Hilliard also argued that there were two reasons for knowing the African heritage in education, child raising, and socialization. He said that "we have the best teaching and socialization practices ever developed and the primary tool of our oppression is mis-education." Hilliard's main contention was that teaching had to be seen as a sacred work because the teacher had to tap into the spiritual realm to focus on making the community better through the positive teaching of children. The African teacher cannot see the children as clients or customers; they must see them as the continuation of a divine work.

In several of his speeches, Hilliard (1998) declared that the proper orientation for teachers had to be, among other things, the beliefs that the cosmos is alive, that spirituality is the center of our being, that African people have a divine purpose and destiny, that each child is a living sun, that children can move toward perfection to be more like the Creator, that *Maat* should be the focus of the curriculum, that knowledge of self is the premium knowledge, that mastery is possible and desirable, that the genius and divinity of children are reflected in intellect, humanity, and spirit, and that teaching is itself a calling toward mastery. Hilliard had arrived at these conclusions after a long career as dean of education at San Francisco State University and distinguished professor at Georgia State University. Finally, in one of his most influential articles, he wrote,

> There is rather a brutal pessimism which permeates the expectations of too many of us; those on the front lines, and those in more remote policy positions—perhaps even those in the general public at large. We have adjusted to very low levels of performance from children in the schools; now it takes very little to satisfy us. (Hilliard, 1991, p. 31)

For the past two decades, my writing and research have been focused on pedagogical success in two areas. On the one hand, I continue to be intrigued and exhilarated by educators who are winning magnificently—that is, educators who are able to teach so that the masses of students they teach have excellent performance. At the same time, I am fascinated and exhilarated when I have the opportunity to observe those magnificent teacher-educators who are able to transfer their knowledge of excellent teaching to raw recruits.

In spite of the changes in perception among educators that have come about because of the Effective Schools movement, I believe that we are yet to be captured by a vision of an excellent school movement. For too many educators, such a goal seems closer to fantasy than reality. As a result, I have tried to highlight many examples of excellence in teaching and teacher education in the hope that they would be noticed by a broad audience and emulated where possible. Teaching and research should begin in most instances from an examination of power teaching.

Barbara A. Sizemore dedicated her life to a revolutionary pedagogy where children were taught to learn but not forced to learn at a certain speed. "It is not so much how fast a child reads but whether or not a child reads at any rate," Sizemore (2008, p. 28) said.

Jawanza Kunjufu (1985) argued that Black boys were under threat almost from the time they entered school and there needed to be a stronger attempt to rescue boys from the damage caused by the education system.

Joyce King (1991) wrote about narratives of memory and shows us how an Afrocentric pedagogy can lean toward revolution. She believed that education is what is being done now. There is no education but that which is being practiced.

While it is easy to say that the scientific revolution brought into being the separation of value and fact, matter and spirit, it is not so easy to see how the European Enlightenment and the scientific revolution dealt with racist myths. One might even say that the European Enlightenment represented the height of European notions of superiority and hence was among the most backward moments in European history despite the propaganda to the contrary.

The goals of a revolutionary pedagogy are clear. In revolutionary pedagogy, we seek to make children appreciate their own histories and cultures as integrated into all systems of knowing. That is, children must not feel when they leave your class that they are outside of the subject you are teaching. The revolutionary teacher pulls the child into the circle of the subject.

The revolutionary pedagogist demands that students are aware of other ethnic and cultural groups and their contributions to human knowledge. I deliberately use the term "pedagogist" in a new way so as to unhinge it from the Greek idea of a young male slave supervising the children of the master, which is usually rendered as "pedagogue." The pedagogist is a conscious interpreter of the signs and symbols that constitute the educational architecture of a society. In fact, a pedagogist is not merely a supervisor but an active participant in the construction of a revolutionary knowledge. This means that revolutionary pedagogists must search out the information that will allow them to wield this incredible power in the classroom.

Revolutionary pedagogy obliterates cultural ignorance at every turn by employing the techniques of transmitting knowledge based on facts, with an eye toward the community values of truth, order, balance, harmony, justice, and reciprocity.

A revolutionary pedagogy is therefore a projection of the will to be human among other humans and to protect the legacies of humanity. Nothing is easy about this, but it is achievable when teachers are good people transmitting information. The revolutionary teacher is just such a person, gifted with knowledge of a particular subject, filled with an inexhaustible passion for teaching, and willing to demonstrate techniques that bring all students into the arena of human achievement.

In the American context, one thing has been clear as long as the society has had educational institutions and that is that those institutions were never designed primarily as sites for Black education. In other words, Black people were never seen as the source and origin of the process. No school system, for example, was designed with African American students as the primary subjects. That is precisely why we have had so many "correctives" intended to adjust the education system, the curriculum, and the pedagogy for Black children, and indeed, for all children other than White children. This is a problem for all teachers and students, and it remains one of the overwhelming issues to be confronted by revolutionary pedagogy. Mwalimu Shujaa (1994) describes what he calls the oppressive nature of schooling in his book, *Too Much Schooling, Too Little Education: The Paradox of Black Lives in White Societies.* "Education is our means of providing for the inter-generational transmission of values, beliefs, traditions, customs, rituals and sensibilities along with the knowledge of why these things must be sustained" (p. 1). Shujaa is essentially criticizing the way Black children have been educated in American society.

A horrendous record of miseducation of Black children confronts every school district in the United States. Our children are suffering under a reign of intellectual terrorism where most teachers cannot identify five African ethnic groups brought to the Americas during the enslavement era. So problematic is this terrorism that we are forced to witness the slow destruction of our students' brains as information about the diaspora is woefully lacking in schools. If you were to ask students in high school to name the country in the Americas with the largest populations of Africans, few would be able to give a good guess, so tragic is the lack of information about the European slave trade in our public schools.

I think that the only way to achieve any sense of revolutionary direction in pedagogy is to reorient toward a new emphasis on proper content. For example, if a teacher is going to teach about Africa, she should teach about all of Africa and dispense with the old broken formula of Africa south of the Sahara or the use of sub-Saharan terms. The Sahara is a desert on the continent of Africa, just as the Mojave is a desert in the country of the United States. Breaking the back of the orthodoxy will require a commitment to a new regime of knowledge.

Consequently, revolutionary pedagogy must no longer teach children about a geographical area called the Middle East. This is not just bad geography, it is politics and has no fundamental relationship to the truth about anything in Africa. There is no middle-eastern part of Africa. Indeed, the idea of the Middle East is a 20th century phenomenon established in the literature after the founding of the state of Israel. In one swell swoop, so to speak, writers could speak of Israel and its Arab neighbors as living in the Middle East. Technically, this term does not stand a chance of survival in revolutionary pedagogy because to be in the "middle east" actually depends on where you start your visualization. In fact, to the Chinese, Germany might be the Middle East. It is said that the sun rises in the east and sets in the west, but the east and the west are always changing as the sun races across the sky. Revolutionary pedagogists will abandon the idea of the Middle East because it is a testament to Eurocentric conceptualizations of space.

As far as we know now, human beings as *Homo sapiens* originated in East Africa, somewhere between Ethiopia and Tanzania. And since that time, *Homo sapiens* have been balancing commonalities and diversities with unending periods of great tension, stress, and warfare, seeking to right the perceived slights and wrongs of other humans. There has rarely been a period of time on the earth when humans have been completely free of conflict. Although conflicts might not exist in one area of the world at a point in time, they are sure to exist in another during the same period as the season of peace in the first area.

PRACTICE BREAKING BARRIERS

Most children in the United States have a negative view of Africa. Africans do not base such a perception of Africa on anything they have read in books; these perceptions most likely arise from media sources and general historic ignorance about the continent. How to break the myths as we would break a toothpick is the question. A teacher can simply introduce new information and evidence that contradicts the old myth. This is probably the most direct way to challenge false ideas.

Once again, the revolutionary pedagogist seeks to unravel all forms of twisted thinking about Africa to prepare the groundwork for inspiring good performance, attracting interest, and attaching students to content. I once sat in a classroom in a large metropolitan city in the Midwest as the teacher told the students about lions and tigers in the African jungle. I wanted to go through the floor because I just knew that at any moment a student would jump up and say, "Ms. Caroline, there are no tigers in Africa." No student caught the misstatement, and Ms. Caroline did not seem to realize that tigers are Asian animals. Later, I gave her that information and then told her that "jungle" is not a good identification of the topography of Africa. The continent is mostly grassland and rainforest, and neither classifies as jungle.

Clearly. the notion that Africa is dangerous circulates among teachers, schools, universities, and other institutions. It is very difficult to break this myth, but it must be broken. There are so many young people from Europe, the Americas, and Asia now traveling around the continent with no major concern about safety because, unless you happen upon a war, there is no place in Africa where you have to fear the local population. The general African idea about human beings is that they are human until they prove that they are *inhuman*.

I find that most people who live in Africa do not find it too dangerous, too hot, or too damp for human beings to survive. It is a much-loved continent, so much so that whites who have settled in Kenya, South Africa, the Ivory Coast, or Namibia do not want to leave. Some areas of Africa are deeply urban and have long histories of urbanization; hence, cities such as Lagos and Kinshasa, now considered two of the most populated cities in the world with more than 25 million people, or Cape Town, Durban, Johannesburg, Nairobi, Abidjan, Dakar, and Addis Ababa are as sophisticated as any cities you will find on any other continent. To some degree, this is a function of global capital that cannot be underestimated in producing similar technologies around the world, but on the other hand, Africans have approached the new situation with African sentiments, aesthetics, and sensibilities.

The history of Africa is long; the history of humans in Africa is the longest in the world. It is interesting that there are still people insisting that Africa has no history. This Hegelian notion has refused to die, although it has been assaulted for the past 60 years by some of the best African minds. Cheikh Anta Diop, Theophile Obenga, Teshale Tibebu, and others have demonstrated that Hegel's original idea in 1828 about Africa having no history was maliciously wrong. What is history anyway? Who gets to tell the narrative, and who gets to record it? How is it propagated, and who subscribes to it? These are all questions about power and the revolutionary pedagogist must bring these issues up in the classroom.

I once thought that the classroom should be free of difficult ideas, but if one is not able to discuss difficult ideas in the classroom—and really, if you think about it, these are not difficult ideas—then where are we to discuss them? Why do you think we have such illiteracy among adults who can read? Literacy cannot be just about knowing your ABCs; it must be about knowing how to change your life because you understand concepts and ideas.

Critical thinking is now considered a base rock for educational thinking, yet it is hardly the kind of critical thinking that will help African American children. Raise questions that are pointed to their history and culture. In the 1990s, a teacher at a small school near Philadelphia was telling his class that the only people who ever domesticated elephants were Indians from Asia when a young girl of about 14 years stood up and asked him, "Isn't it true that Hannibal's army trained elephants to cross the Alps?" The teacher did not know how to answer the student, and rather than saying, "Let me look into that," he simply repeated that only Indian elephants were trainable. Doubling down never means that you are right; it is like an ostrich digging its head deeper into the ground. The answer to the question is "Yes, Hannibal the Great, of African Khart Haddas, often called Carthage, led his elephants over the Alps to fight the Romans."

Another myth is that all Africans are the same. When people say or think this, it is important to know what they mean. There are nearly 3,000 languages spoken on the continent of Africa, making it the most diverse continent on earth. To say that all Africans are the same is to not take into consideration the immense diversity of histories, heroics, travel, adventure, politics, art, culture, and religion on the continent. Even with this diversity, however, there are certain common traits found among African ethnic groups. Usually, scholars say that most Africans have a special place for ancestor reverence in their philosophical systems. This means that whether one is from Ghana in West Africa or South Africa or Kenya there are certain values that tend to be similar. So one has to say that common values exist but different histories also exist. The Zulu and the Asante people are not the same in their specific histories, but they both share a common approach to ancestors.

Here are 10 common value systems found throughout Africa:

1. The most important value is respect and reverence for one's ancestors.
2. Character is the greatest virtue in a relationship.
3. Fertility in the sense of reproduction is a high value.
4. Collective and communal values are consistent in African societies.
5. Discovering one's destiny and living it is important.
6. Agrarian values dominate most societies.
7. African societies are evolving toward community harmony.
8. Children are weaned late.
9. Music and dance are of the same fabric.
10. Respect for elders is an important virtue.

Using these values in lesson plans or as a foundation for discussing academic subjects and themes in classrooms is a way to support revolutionary pedagogy. What is intended by listing these values is that the teacher will have solid African cultural values to explore in building classroom discourse. Take the ideal of respect for elders among many African communities, and you will see that this ideal can be evaluated and utilized in social studies classes. Teach this ethic as a way to respect one's peers. Revolutionary pedagogists will sometimes ask that students bring their grandparents or great-aunts and great-uncles to the school classroom to engage in cultural remembering conversations. Stories told by elders are often quite striking and motivating to students. In revolutionary pedagogy, it is often said, "Let the elders speak!" Consequently, encouraging elders to visit the classroom and recount their experiences is a way to build community solidarity and to impart values by demonstration.

CHAPTER 5
Essential Knowledge for Revolutionary Teachers

Teachers Do the Best They Can

Teachers teach what they know. It is to be expected that teachers will not be able to teach what they do not know. In fact, some teachers actually do not want to know what it is that they do not know. Yet to be an effective teacher, there are some assumptions that a teacher of African American, Native American, Latin American, and Asian American children needs to embrace. I do not mention European-descended students only because they are the default group in American education.

One of the key aspects of teaching is knowing who it is you are teaching. If you do not know the children sitting in the classroom, you will not be consistently successful as a teacher. Who are these children? Are they in good fettle? What do they eat for breakfast, or do they eat at all? What kinds of families do they come from, or are they living with guardians? What kind of music do they listen to, and what excites them about popular culture? What are they expected to know about your topic?

Answering as many of these questions as you can prior to teaching a class will help tremendously. In fact, at some level, the teacher might be able to catch up with this information by asking some of the less embarrassing questions on the first day of class. The revolutionary pedagogist never forgets that the main goal is to get the student to learn. A teacher is not a teacher until the pupil has learned. This is why analyzing the classroom affords the teacher an advantage over those teachers who assume that they know what they are talking about and do not need any analysis.

First, teachers must understand that they do not know everything they need to know to be able to teach the children in their classrooms. This does not mean that you do not know your subject, one for which you have paid dearly in time and effort as well as money to acquire; it simply means that there are cultural and historical artifacts that you do not know. Learning is pragmatic and demonstrative for the student; the teacher must model that behavior and not have closed eyes or a closed mind.

Second, the teacher must realize that students attend to what they are interested in and this is the best approach to attaching them to the subject. Gaining the attention of students and having them participate in learning is a technique that must be studied and practiced with patience and humility. Attracting students to a topic or theme depends on a combination of pedagogical skills that are attainable through knowledge. *The principal rule of revolutionary pedagogy is that all classroom behaviors are controlled through superior knowledge.* The teacher who is willing to submit to such knowledge can and will be very successful in the classroom. I will lay this out more clearly in the following pages.

Third, the teacher, to be revolutionary, must challenge all orthodoxies when the situations in the classroom demand it. This is not challenge for the sake of obstruction, deviance, or comedy but for seizing moments for knowledge intervention. The best teachers are those who can understand how to challenge the canards of practice and create innovation, interest, and color in the classroom. Students appreciate teachers who teach differently just because those teachers are the ones who do not think that there is something wrong with the new generation. They embrace revolution.

WHAT TEACHERS NEED TO UNDERSTAND ABOUT EDUCATION

In revolutionary pedagogy, we look for teachers who are able to understand the great diversity of our students. I have simplified the process by suggesting that we need to study the ideas of perspective, agency, and location. These are fundamental tools of Afrocentric education, and as useful concepts in teaching, they have the potential to be revolutionary. We generally say that the idea of perspective leans in different directions depending on your view of the world. Afrocentrists tend to value openness, straightforwardness, trust, and consistency when it comes to evaluating a situation, judging a fact, or responding to an individual. On the other hand, it is suggested that whites' perspective may conjure up that which is secret, duplicitous, suspicious, and inconsistent.

Moving to agency, the Afrocentrist seeks collective actualizing and is motivated by shame, openness, and personal relations, as opposed to the more Eurocentric idea of individual actualizing, guilt, secrecy, and impersonal relationships. Each of these represents values that we find in our society. Ultimately, we have to proclaim centeredness, trust, and balance as opposed to absolute fluidity, suspicion, and being unsettled.

Given this set of binaries, homologies, and antipathies, it should not be a surprise to discover that this bifurcation extends to our concept of society as well. African people have met Europeans in many spheres and over the past 500 years have experienced an inordinate amount of the most aggressive human greed and brutality. Most of Europe cannot teach us society, civilization, democracy, law, ethics, human relations, or values; its history has been the antithesis of those ideas. Africans gave the world the full meaning of the concept of freedom from oppression. Two hundred and forty-six years of enslavement gave a warrant to Africans to make freedom the hallmark of struggle. In every era and at all times, African Americans have had to confront agency reduction formations in all sectors of the society. Education is no exception as a locus of confrontation where African Americans are up against curriculum and pedagogy that act to reduce agency.

Learning to Recognize Dysconscious Racism

Joyce King (1991) said that dysconscious racism "denotes the limited and distorted understanding students have about inequity and cultural diversity—understandings that make it difficult for them to act in favor of truly equitable education" (p. 134). A revolutionary pedagogist must learn to recognize dysconscious racism, that is, situations where teachers may not have the intention of practicing racism but the results of their behaviors, methods, and temperaments are nevertheless just as if they were based on racial animosity. King saw situations where teachers might discover that their White students might be threatened emotionally by Afrocentric infusion methods, a liberatory curriculum, or a revolutionary pedagogy teacher-educator. In such cases, King, one of the most progressive educators in America, suggested that the teacher might need to reconstruct social knowledge and self-identity. Of course, the reconstruction may not happen until teachers realize that they are agitated by the new information. It would be best if the teacher education program or professional development program could prepare teachers to confront this possibility in themselves or in their students prior to the classroom experience.

As a practical matter, I have always felt that the best method of steeling the teacher against dysconscious racism is to teach the teacher how to recognize and deal with oppression. King goes so far as to elevate this idea alongside reconstruction of self-identity as a technique to deal with dysconscious racism. If you cannot identify oppression, then you will not be able to combat it in your classroom. For the revolutionary pedagogist, identification and treatment of dysconscious racism are important to the process of bringing into existence an authentic revolutionary pedagogy.

If a teacher is unable to identify racism or color privilege, then that teacher will have a difficult time in an urban classroom. Some teachers participate in dysconscious racism because they are clueless about racial oppression. I do not believe that these teachers are necessarily racist themselves, but they are participants in dysconscious racism. What one hopes is that such teachers would study various situations to gain a more empathetic understanding of how racism in all of its forms has challenged students culturally, ethically, and politically.

Appreciating the Classical African Philosophy of Learning

It goes without saying that most educators are familiar with the various theories and theorists of education in the Western world. It is common to hear teachers speak of John Dewey's pragmatism, Hegelian ideas, and social Darwinism as aspects of European intellectual thought. Primarily because we have been trained in the West, which is extremely high on itself, we know the Greek influence on education and have some understanding of how Greece and Rome, that is, Greek and Latin, played major roles in European education. We know next to nothing about how classical Africa created initiations, rituals of excellence, disciplinary study, and methods of transmission of information to disciples. To be effective as a revolutionary pedagogist, the teacher must appreciate the origin of African history and knowledge.

Herodotus, Clement of Alexandria, and Diodorus, three ancient Greeks among others, claimed that the ancient Africans of Egypt had six specific grades of students. The levels of education, in some way or another, represented the paths of initiates toward higher and higher information found in other African societies. Students had to master the knowledge in a particular grade before they could move on; in effect, Africans laid the foundation for the class or grade levels we now find in most educational systems. Students had to master certain books of Tehuti, often called by the Greeks, Hermes or Thoth. According to Clement, as reported by George James (2014) in *Stolen Legacy*, the description of the order of priestly education in the Egyptian Mysteries went as follows:

First comes the singer *Odus*, bearing an instrument of music. He has to know by heart two of the books of Tehuti; one containing the hymns of the Gods, and the other, the allotment of the king's life. Next comes the *Horoscopus*, carrying in his hand a horologium or sun-dial, and a palm branch; the symbols of Astronomy. He has to know four of the books of Hermes, which deal with Astronomy. Next comes the *Hierogrammat*, with feathers on his head, and a book in his hand, and a rectangular case with writing materials, i.e., the writing ink and the reed. He has to know the hieroglyphics, cosmography, geography, astronomy, the topography of Egypt, the sacred utensils and measures, the temple furniture and the lands. Next comes the *Stolistes*, carrying the cubit of justice, and the libation vessels. He has to know the books of Hermes that deal with the slaughter of animals. Next comes the *Prophetes* carrying the vessel of water, followed by those who carry the loaves. The *Prophetes* has to know the ten books that are called hieratic, and contain the laws and doctrines concerning the secret theology (Gods-theology) and the whole education of the Priests. The books of Hermes are 42 in number and are absolutely necessary. 36 of them have to be known by the Orders that precede and contain the whole philosophy of the Egyptians. The remaining six books must be known by the Order of *Pastophori*. These are medical books and deal with physiology, male and female diseases, anatomy, drugs and instruments. The books of Hermes were well known to the ancient world and were known to Clement of Alexandria, who lived at the beginning of the third century A.D. (p. 96)

Six Levels of Ancient Egyptian Education

These six levels, *odus, horoscopus, hierogrammat, stolistes, prophetes,* and *pastophori*, encompassed a complete curriculum for those who would teach others. In the West, the educational system has evolved to the point where a student who would be a teacher simply majors in a field and then takes certain practical courses in education that assist with the preparation of course outlines, lesson plans, and alignments to certain standards set by the state or institution. Obviously, this type of education is not designed in a revolutionary manner; the aim of this structure is to maintain the status quo, not to overturn it or to disturb the student's cocoon. Revolutionary pedagogy aims to bring about a transformation in the information and in the presentation of that information, and transformation of the teacher, making the teacher subscribe personally to a revolutionary agenda. I want nothing more than for a student to walk out of your classroom and say, "I have learned something that I had not even thought about, but I know I will never be the same after this class!" This is not an uncommon statement even among students who have not been consistently exposed to revolutionary materials, but it can be even more common and less stressful if you think of teaching as a subversive act because you are trying to move students off of the old terms.

BEGINNING THE LESSON WITH THE BEGINNING

I was never very fond of remembering dates when I was an elementary and high school student. Somehow the rote memorizing of dates seemed pointless to my young mind; it would be many decades before I appreciated the value of dates. Increasingly, over the years, I have concluded that the most important aspect of the lesson plan is the starting place, and that is what my teachers did not understand. I would have been much farther along in critical thinking had I mastered the understanding of the beginning.

Revolutionary pedagogy demands that a teacher start with origins and definitions because this is where one sets the stage for a child to learn in context. If you do not have a sense of time, it will be hard to establish a location, and without a location in the subject field, you may end up with distorted information. Consequently, a person could be studying cell theory in biology and not know that among the first scientists to write about cell theory was the African American Ernest Just in the 1940s. Knowing biology is one thing, but knowing that Just was an early pioneer in a specific field of biology allows students, of all backgrounds, to appreciate the primacy of Just's discoveries. Without this understanding, a teacher may teach biology without being able to attach the African American child to the subject. I think it is a good exercise for teachers to explore all the possibilities for connections to their students even if it takes a little more time. There is nothing that humans have done for a long time that other humans have not been able to do. So giving the origins and the definitions of concepts goes hand in hand with revolutionary pedagogy.

ASSUMPTIONS OF A REVOLUTIONARY PEDAGOGY

Teachers rarely get the training they need for revolutionary pedagogy; that is why professional development for teachers is essential. Any school district or school that tries to get ahead without some development work with teachers will fail. It is impossible to teach in urban school districts, whether Atlanta or Detroit, San Francisco or San Antonio, without some solid culturally relevant training, preferably in revolutionary pedagogy. Here are three foundational blocks of revolutionary pedagogy:

1. Human beings originated on the African continent.
2. All human migration to other parts of the world started from Africa.
3. The originators of geometry, sculpture, medicine, philosophy, and astronomy were Africans.

The reader may be thinking, "Why is it necessary to state these assumptions?" It is necessary mainly because there are many people who still believe that these assumptions are false, contrary to the reports of all scientists. Nevertheless, for revolutionary pedagogy, you must know and accept these assumptions because without them everything that comes after will seem confusing and contradictory. We must argue for the right of students to be taught from the standpoint of their own agency. This depends on knowledge of the origin and migration of humans and other factors in the development and emergence of knowledge.

The Origin and Migration of Humans

As far as scientists know, *Homo sapiens* originated in East Africa and spread to the rest of the earth. It is fair to say that before 70,000 years ago all humans were Black. Leaving Africa, *Homo sapiens* made it to the ends of the earth in less than 30,000 years. When civilization took hold in the Nile River valley, numerous people from Uganda to the Mediterranean Sea added to the narrative of society. Writing, medicine, architecture, the domestication of animals, the naming of the stars, the creation of the calendar, and mathematics became formidable foundations for all knowledge. The educator who can lock in this information will be able to appreciate the lesson plans that will attach the student to contemporary subjects.

Unsung Names From African History

I have chosen to write the names of some Africans that you may have not heard of but are integral to an understanding and appreciation of African culture and history. Teachers should master several of these names in terms of their historical narrative and their place in world history. Each one of these names can generate discussion, ideas, and visions. Allow students to research the names, make their own narratives about the names, and discuss them in class. It is alright if several students choose the same name.

Menes: The African king who united 42 communities along the Nile River

Imhotep: African builder of the first pyramid and the first physician in history

Amenhotep, son of Hapu: Ancient African who was considered the person "who knew all there was to know"

Ramses II: One of the greatest African monarchs in history and the builder of many monuments

Nefertari: Favorite wife of Ramses II, for whom he built a temple at Abu Simbel

Thutmoses III: The African who was the greatest conquering king in history

Hatshepsut: The most prominent African female leader in the ancient world

Queen Tiye: The African woman who influenced many leaders of the 18th dynasty

Taharka: One of the greatest African leaders, who united Kemet with Nubia

Cheikh Anta Diop: Considered the greatest African intellectual of the 20th century

W. E. B. Du Bois: Author of 33 books and the most distinguished African American intellectual of the 20th century

Nat Turner: Iconic leader of the 1831 revolt against slavery

Ahmad Baba: Author of 42 books and the last chancellor of the University of Sankore in Timbuktu

Cheikh Omar Tall: Born in Futa Toro in the late 18th century, one of the most important generals to fight against the French

Kwame Nkrumah: The greatest proponent of Pan Africanism and the first president of Ghana

Amadou Bamba: The spiritual leader of the Mourrides brotherhood in Senegal

Sundiata: The noblest name in the gallery of West African empire builders

Nzingha: The queen who led her armies against the Portuguese in the Congo and Angola region

Hintsa kaKhawuta: The 13th king of the amaXhosa nation, who led the most powerful kingdom in the Eastern Cape

Shaka kaSenzangakhona: The great Zulu king who created a mighty martial nation in the early 19th century in southern Africa

Paul Robeson: African American singer and a civil rights spokesperson in the 20th century

Nanny of the Maroons: A Jamaican national hero who was a leader of the Maroons, who fought the English colonialists in the 18th century

Zumbi: African Brazilian hero associated with the quilombo that claimed independence from the Portuguese colonialists

Paul Bogle: Jamaican national hero who fought for the legitimate rights of Blacks in Jamaica

Dessalines: Haitian who defeated Napoleon's army in 1804

Abubakari: Malian king who sent hundreds of ships toward the Americas in 1311–1312

Abdias do Nascimento: The most important African Brazilian intellectual and social rights leader of the 20th century

Booker T. Washington: Founder of Tuskegee Institute

Mary McLeod Bethune: Founder of Bethune-Cookman College and the National Council of Negro Women

Nelson Mandela: The first democratically elected president of South Africa

Yanga: African who led a revolt against the Spanish in Mexico

Manuel Zapata Olivella: One of the most important African Colombian writers of the 20th century

Mansa Musa: The African emperor who has been called "the richest man in the history of the world"

Vicente Guerrero: The first Mexican president who was the first African-descendant president of a North American country

Barack Obama: The first African American president in the United States

Kwame Ture: One of the most popular leaders of the Student Nonviolent Coordinating Committee

Marcus Garvey: Heroic leader of the Universal Negro Improvement Association and the African Communities League who organized 10 million Blacks

Langston Hughes: One of the greatest poets of the Harlem Renaissance period

Nicolas Guillen: African Cuban poet who was the national poet laureate of Cuba

Menelik II: The powerful Ethiopian emperor who defeated the Italian army at Adwa

Hannibal Barca: African king who led Khart-Haddas against Rome during the 3rd century BCE

These are just a few of the names that teachers who teach Black children should know as a matter of course. The comments are truncated, and I hope that the revolutionary pedagogist will add to this information or have students research these individuals and others. Understanding and appreciating the use of these names and the histories and dramas that come with them would greatly enrich the teaching experience and bring the student into the context of your topic, whatever it is! You could experiment by classifying these names and others into philosophers, scientists, poets, military leaders, and resistance fighters. Add to the list, and have students research others that should be added. This list is merely suggestive.

AFRICAN-DESCENDED WRITERS IN THE WORLD

Writers of African heritage have been heralded in many countries. Alexander Pushkin in Russia, Alexander Dumas and Aimé Cesaire in France, Langston Hughes and Toni Morrison in the United States, and Nicolas Guillen in Cuba have demonstrated enormous capacities in language and culture. Have students research these names and report on them in class. Identify their qualities of character, discipline, and hard work and emphasize this to the class. This list is not complete, but each teacher can add to the list from African and African American history books. There are books on inventors, astronauts, and the Egyptian philosophers. Most of the Egyptian philosophers lived before the Greeks and achieved lasting recognition in Greece because Greeks like Thales, Anaxagoras, Plato, Eudoxos, Anaxamander, Isocrates, and Pythagoras went to school in Africa. Pythagoras spent 22 years in Egypt. Africans called the land Kemet, and later the Greeks referred to it as Egypt.

CORRECTING WHAT'S WRONG IN EDUCATION

- There is something wrong with a society that does not teach students how to understand their past.
- There is something wrong with an education that causes the oppressed to imitate their oppressors in values and narratives.
- There is something wrong with a society that cannot overcome the ignorance of racism even when people are educated in its schools.

I do not advocate the position that the past was better than the future, nor am I encouraging teachers to live in the past. I simply suggest that studying the past allows us to choose what was good and to avoid what was bad in the past. African pedagogy from the time of the Mystery Schools in Egypt to the current schools where children learn by doing is grounded in spiritual values. The question of education is "How does one become a good person?" Or in some societies, "How does one become human?" These are not considered relevant questions in education today, and consequently we see that children who go through the American system often end up narcissistic and materialistic. African pedagogy is involved in socialization of the child; in the West, socialization of the child is left to other institutions, some social and some religious.

As soon as a woman becomes pregnant in many African societies, the entire village begins the process of education for prenatal socialization. Once the infant is born, the village participates in the postnatal socialization process. Nothing is left to chance. The aim is to foster the intense bonding of the mother and child so that everyone knows what is to be expected and what is to be done. Reciprocity is considered a part of the process of learning in community, and certain spaces are set aside for this type of ritual. The child grows up in a community where all the people are for the child and the child is for all the people. These spaces are designated at times as sacred places. While one cannot repeat or imitate all of the bonding of a mother and a child in revolutionary pedagogy, we suggest that the teacher becomes someone who discovers places or times, or both, that are special, sacred in other words, for the students. It might be the library or a table in the back of the classroom. This is not a space for punishment but for reflection, recovery, or reading. My eighth-grade teacher, Mrs. Austin, would let me spend time in the library reading for 30 minutes if she wanted to make a point about me having done exceptionally well in class. I truly appreciated that recognition and time. She would often stop by to see what I was reading. Students remember those occasions and will work hard to keep that bonding. We call these practices rituals for a reason. They are not like other moments or spaces because they provide an opportunity to

- share knowledge;
- share symbols;
- reinforce social bonds;
- use art, music, and reading;
- employ games, if possible, to integrate knowledge; and
- celebrate in a way that allows the community to mark distinction.

Engaging in this type of revolutionary pedagogy will help us break the sieves through which urban children pass into the stream of negativity. Among these negative sieves used as crippling tools against African American children are special education, compensatory education, boot camp for violent children, vouchers, choice for the affluent to abandon the public schools, and direct instruction for poor and low-achieving students. The revolutionary pedagogist insists on removing these stresses on the education experience by teaching children with a new pedagogy that recognizes and honors their agency to assert themselves while demonstrating an antiracist ethic.

CHAPTER 6

Revolutionary Illustrations and Demonstrations

Joyce E. King says, "Critical, transformative teachers must develop a pedagogy of social action and advocacy that really celebrates diversity, not just random holidays, isolated cultural artifacts, or 'festivals and food'" (p. 134). In this assessment, King is following Bill Ayers's argument in his 1988 article "Young Children and the Problem of the Color Line" in *Democracy and Education*. Ayers, a prominent educator, contends that the public school system is much too rigid and hostile toward creativity and much too bureaucratic and rigid for effective education. In Ayers's view, the educational system normally structures learning in ways that prevent independent thinking. Ayers has campaigned for years to secure respect for the individual growth of each student. Like the revolutionary pedagogists, Ayers questions the classification of students based on standardized tests rather than on human creativity, thus encouraging and supporting a transformative philosophy of education.

Both King and Ayers occupy key positions in the ranks of progressive educators who seek to extend democracy in school systems. They understand the need for illustrative and demonstrative materials to assist teachers in getting up to speed in revolutionary pedagogy.

I will present here several illustrative and demonstrative examples that might be used in explaining and interpreting facts, themes, conditions, environments, and personalities in education. An illustration is an example, often accompanied by an image or picture, that is used to clarify something. A demonstration is an act of providing evidence to show the truth of a certain idea, argument, or concept. It may or may not be augmented by an illustration. If we are to improve the dissemination of knowledge and the distribution of democracy in education, we must also create opportunities for revolutionary pedagogy by giving teachers the best tools possible.

My aim here is to show teachers who want to be revolutionary pedagogists what to use (and how to use it) to establish a mode of instruction that would recenter dislocated African American students and expand the knowledge of all other students in the classroom. Here are a few themes and pedagogical scaffolds that will assist the teacher who is seeking ways to approach important topics.

THE ENSLAVEMENT OF AFRICANS IN AMERICA

The enslavement of Africans has been one of the most difficult areas for teachers to cover adequately. In revolutionary pedagogy, the teacher must become an active participant in raising the consciousness of students about the horrors and evils of the enslavement. So how do you teach about the enslavement of Africans? One must do it as one would teach about the Holocaust. Those who created the institution of chattel slavery, like those who created the conditions for the Holocaust, did so out of a belief that the victims were less than the perpetrators in terms of human value. The enslavement of Africans was a crime against humanity and can never be supported in any way. There are no silver or gold linings in the inimical clouds of depravity that produced the horrendous bondage of millions of people.

Since we have few written records by Africans during the enslavement, how do we teach about the enslavement? The revolutionary pedagogist must use what is available. For example, we know that announcements of runaways were common because Africans ran away from the plantations and farms quite regularly. Whites placed advertisements in newspapers seeking to have whites in the public capture and return runaway Africans to enslavement. Those ads can become primary evidence about the lifestyles, dress, attitudes, histories, courage, families, and intelligence of the enslaved Africans. For example, in the newspaper ads below, I have followed each one with questions that might be discussed, descriptions that might be investigated, and attitudes that might demonstrate the state of mind of Africans in resistance to enslavement.

Using 18th Century Runaway African Advertisements as Heuristics

May 5, 1738. Ran away from the Subscriber's Quarters on Sapponic, in Prince George County, 14 or 15 Weeks ago, a Mulattoe Man Slave, named Tom, 25 Years old, about 5 feet 8 or 9 Inches high, thin faced, and bushy Hair, if not cut off; he is very apt to grin when he speaks, or is spoken to; had on an old dark Fustian Coat, with plain yellow Metal Buttons; Hath been several Times taken up, and escaped again before he could be deliver'd to the Quarter whereunto he belon'd; and the last Time shackled, Handcuffed, and an Iron Collar about his Neck, with Prongs, and to some of them Links. Whoever will deliver him to me, in Charles-City County, shall have a Pistole Reward, besides what the law allows; and if brought from any great Distance a farther Reward suitable to the Trouble, by

John Stith

N.B. It is suspected he will endeavour to escape on Board some Vessel.

Questions

1. What is a mulatto? What were the origins of mulatto populations during slavery?
2. What is a "Fustian Coat"? How would an enslaved person have gotten such a coat?
3. Considering, the fact that Tom had escaped and been captured several times before, including "the last Time shackled, Handcuffed, and an Iron Collar about his Neck, with Prongs, and to some of them Links," what do you think was his attitude about his bondage?
4. What does it say about Tom's intelligence that he might "endeavour" to escape on board a boat?

May 2, 1766. Run away from the subscriber, in Mecklenburg county on Wednesday last, a fellow named Jack. It appears he has been principally concerned in promoting the late disorderly meetings among the Negroes, and is gone off for fear of being prosecuted for many robberies he has committed. He is a low squat made fellow, bow-legged, his eyes remarkably red, has been branded on the right cheek R, and on the left M, though not easily to be perceived. It is supposed he intends for Carolina or Georgia. Whoever apprehends the said slave, and will deliver him to me, shall receive 50s. If taken 50 miles from home and 6d [pence] a mile for a greater distance.

Robert Munford

Questions

1. What does it say about Jack's courage that "it appears he has been principally concerned in promoting the late disorderly meetings among the Negroes"?
2. What would be considered "disorderly meetings" in your judgment? Discuss this with the students.
3. What "robberies" by Jack, which is the taking of "property" from the slaveholder, would be greater than his escape? Discuss the idea of chattel slavery.
4. Find out how much 50 shillings would have been during that period.
5. Speak about his physical traits and the branding on his face. Explain the idea of branding of enslaved Africans.

Oct. 10, 1767. Prince George, Sept. 28, 1767. RUN away from the subscriber, the 22d of this instant, three slaves, viz. JUPITER, alias GIBB, a Negro fellow, about 35 years of age, about 6 feet high, knock kneed, flat footed, the right knee bent in more than the left, has several scars on his back from a severe whipping he lately had at Sussex court-house, having been tried there for stirring up the Negroes to an insurrection, being a great Newlight preacher. ROBIN about 25 years of age, a stout fellow, about 6 feet high, has a film over one of his eyes, a sore on one of his shins, and is brother to Gibb. DINAH, an old wench, very large, near

6 feet high; she has a remarkable stump of a thumb, occasioned by a whitlow, by which the bones of the first joint came out and is mother to the two fellows. They carried with them a variety of clothes, among the rest an old blue duffil great coat, one bearskin do, a scarlet jacket, and a fine new linen shirt. It is supposed they will endeavour to make their escape southward. Whoever takes up, and conveys to me the above slave, shall have a reward of 50s. for each of the fellows, and 20s for the wench, if taken in Virginia; if any other government, £5 for each of the fellows, and 40s for the wench paid by

George Noble

Questions

1. What does it say about planning that three enslaved Africans were able to escape at the same time?
2. Explain the relationship between Jupiter, Robin, and Dinah. Discuss the significance of the mother and sons running away together.
3. How could the "severe whipping" have affected Jupiter's willingness to escape?
4. What does it say about Jupiter that he had a role in "stirring up the Negroes to an insurrection"?

Oct. 20, 1768. RUN away from the subscriber in Chesterfield, the Wednesday before Easter last, a bright mulatto wench named Jude, about 30 years old is very remarkable, has lost one eye, but which I have forgot, has long black hair, a large scar on one of her elbows, and several other scars on her face, and has been subject to running away ever since she was ten years old. I have great reason to think she will pass for a free woman, and endeavour to make into South Carolina. She is very knowing about house business, can spin, weave, sew, and iron, well. She had on when she went away her winter clothing, also a blue and white striped Virginia cloth gown, a Virginia cloth coperas and white striped coat, besides others too tedious to mention. Whoever conveys the said slave to me shall be well rewarded for their trouble.

Mary Clay

Questions

1. What might have been Jude's calculation in leaving just before Easter?
2. What was her physical condition? Speculate on how she may have gotten the scars on her body, the lost eye, and the scar on her elbow.
3. Why could she have passed as a free woman?
4. Explain how her knowledge "about house business" could indicate intelligence and provide her skills to escape and live on her own.

May 11, 1769. Run away from the subscriber in Charles City county, the 14th of April last, a VIRGINIA born Negro fellow named PETER, about 44 years of age, of a black complexion, a slim fellow, his teeth cut before as if broke off, and is a sly artful rogue if not watched; he carried with him sundry clothes, such as crop Negroes usually wear, also a white Virginia cloth waistcoat and petticoat, a Tarlton plaid gown, and sundry other of his wife's clothes. He also carried away a gun of an uncommon large size, and a fiddle, which he is much delighted in when he gets any strong drink, which he is remarkably fond of, and then very talkative and impudent. I suspect he has gone to Amelia county, to Mr. Tanner's, as Mrs. Tanner, alias Mrs. Johnson, sold him to Mr. Richard Hayles, and by him sold to the subscriber, as he often told the other Negroes that if ever I used him ill he would go to his old mistress, as she never sold him to Mr. Hayles, but only lent him during pleasure, and that he would go to her and be protected. The said Negro is outlawed; and I will give £10 to any person or persons that will kill him and bring me his head, separate from his body, or 40s. if delivered to the subscriber near the Long Bridge.

William Gregory

Questions

1. Why was Peter considered "a sly artful rogue if not watched"?
2. Explain how those who "sold" him or his ancestors into slavery are not considered "rogues" but the man who escapes is considered such a bad person?
3. Explain what a Tarlton plaid gown is.
4. What are the implications of Peter having a gun? What would the gun be used for?

Oct. 13, 1774. Run away from the Subscriber, last Friday, a likely Virginia born Negro Man called JOHNNY, about 22 Years of Age, five Feet eight Inches high, has a down Look, and Waiter. This Fellow formerly belonged to Armistead Lightfoot, Esq; deceased, and is remarkable for Cock-fighting, Card-playing, and many other Games. I suspect he will pass as a Freeman, and endeavour to get out of the Colony, as he can read and write. All Masters of Vessels are cautioned not to carry him off, at their Peril. I will give 40s. if taken within this Colony and brought home, besides what the Law allows, or £5 if taken in any other Colony.

Charles Grymes

Questions

1. Discuss Johnny's physical condition.
2. Discuss Johnny's ability in organizing and conducting "Cock-fighting, Card-playing, and many other Games." What gave Charles Grymes the idea that Johnny might try to appear as a free man?

June 16, 1775. TEN POUNDS REWARD Run away from the subscriber in Dunmore county, in May last, a negro fellow named SAM. 5 feet 5 or 6 inches high, has a broad face, and is a well looking fellow. As to his clothing, I cannot be certain, he having carried several things with him. He also took with him an old bay horse very gray about the head, an iron pot, a narrow axe, a handsaw, and an old smooth bore gun. About three years ago he purchased his freedom of his old master, Mr. Francis Slaughter, and continued in that state till this spring, when it was discovered he was attempting to inveigle away a number of negroes to the new or Indian country (where he had been most of the last summer) upon which the neighbours insisted on his being reduced to slavery again, and I purchased him. I imagine he will endeavour to pass as a freeman, he having a discharge from his old master, as well as one from Lord Dunmore, having served in the expedition against the Indians last fall. Whoever delivers said slave to me shall have the reward that is offered.

Gabriel Jones

Questions

1. Describe Sam according to this ad, and comment on the fact that the advertisement says he "is a well looking fellow."
2. What does it mean that he was able to take an old bay horse, an iron pot, an axe, a handsaw, and a smooth bore gun? Does this suggest that he was skilled?
3. Why would he have been able to purchase his freedom three years earlier and then become re-enslaved?
4. Claiming that Sam was attempting "to inveigle away a number of negroes to the new or Indian country," the ad suggests that he had been reduced to enslavement again. Discuss Sam's situation as an individual seeking to free himself and others.

Dec. 1, 1774. RUN away from the subscriber in Dinwiddie, the 5th day of April last, a dark mulatto man named JEMMY, 5 feet 9 or 10 inches high, well made, has remarkable long feet, the middle toes longer than the rest, which they ride over, has lost part of one of his foreteeth, which occasions the next to it to look blue, is a very artful fellow, and will probably endeavour to pass for a freeman; he is very fond of singing hymns and preaching, and has been about Williamsburg ever since he went off, passing by the name of James Williams. Whoever apprehends the said slave, and secures him so that I get him again, shall have 40s reward, and if delivered to me in Dinwiddie £4.

David Walker

Questions

1. Who would be a "dark mulatto" man?
2. Jemmy is said to have been "well made," but there was evidence that he had lost one of his front teeth and had long feet. What does it mean that he was "an artful fellow"?
3. Speculate on the possibility that this man may have passed for a free man. How? Why?
4. Jemmy was said to have been fond of "singing hymns and preaching"; what does that say about the readiness of his mind to use all avenues for escape, including religion?

Nov. 29, 1776. RUN away the first of January 1775 a likely mulatto negro wench named Kate, 18 years of age, well made, 5 feet 9 or 10 inches high, and talks very smooth. She was hired to Mr. Philip Moody of Williamsburg in 1774, and last year to Mr. John Thruston, from whence she ran off. She has got a husband in Williamsburg, and probably may pass for a free person as she is well acquainted in that city, and I have repeatedly heard of her being there. She formerly belonged to the estate of Mr. John Cary, deceased, of York county. I will give 20s. to any person that will secure her in jail and give me intelligence thereof, or 40s if brought to me in King & Queen, at Mr. John Thruston's.

EDWARD CARY, jun.

Questions

1. What is the meaning of "wench"? How was she considered "likely"?
2. How do we know that she was intelligent?
3. What does it mean to say that she was passed from one slaveholder to another on three separate occasions?
4. Imagine what her life must have been, and what may have finally driven her away.

RAN away from the subscriber, living on West river, on the 26th of October last, a very likely negro girl named PEGG, she is about fifteen years of age, very black and small for her age, speaks low when spoken to, has been used to wait in the house: had on when she went away an old blue cotton jacket and petticoat, but is probable she got other cloathing since her elopement. The above reward, including what the law allows, will be given to any person apprehending said girl, and securing her in any gaol, so that I get her again, or reasonable charges if brought home, by

Gassaway Pindell

Questions

1. What does this ad say about the age and gender of the person running away?

2. Pegg was small and spoke in quiet tones but yet was able to plan her escape. What could have caused her desire to leave the employ of Gassaway Pindell?

3. What is the meaning of "home" in Pindell's ad?

Finally, remember that these ads were not small in number; there were thousands of them, indicating that Africans were running away from enslavement quite frequently from the earliest of times. Therefore, these ads, while not written by Africans, will give you a lot of information about African people as seen through the eyes of the White slaveholders. If someone was intelligent, bright, clever, artistic, musical, capable of counting, and skilled in performatives of all kinds, the enslaver would most likely have mentioned that in the ad. Study these ads, and reflect on the revolutionary character of your work and the lives of these ancestors.

URBAN TEACHERS AND DEAD WHITE MEN

Why Should White Philosophers Be the Only Ones on the List?

In the 21st century, the vestiges of the racist elements of the Enlightenment must be abandoned, and teachers, especially those taking up the cause of revolutionary pedagogy, must place a new critical eye on all White philosophers. One of the reasons there remains a need for revolutionary pedagogists is that the promotion of White philosophers is probably at the vanguard of all racist thinking. We will never rid the educational system of racist thoughts and ideas until we understand that Hegel, Voltaire, John Locke, Montesquieu, and Thomas Jefferson buttressed the system of white racial supremacy.

In January 2017, students at the University of London's School for Oriental and African Studies protested the teaching of White philosophers. According to the *London Telegraph* writer Camilla Turner (2017), who was reporting on the students' demands, "they say it is part of wider campaign to 'decolonise' the university, as they seek to 'address the structural and epistemological legacy of colonialism'." Teshale Tibebu (2011) argued in his classic study *Hegel and the Third World* that

Hegel, more than any other modern Western philosopher, produced the most systematic case for the superiority of Western White Protestant bourgeois modernity. He established a racially structured ladder of gradation of the peoples of the world, putting Germanic people at the top of the racial pyramid, people of Asia in the middle, and Africans and Indigenous people of the Americas and Pacific Islands at the bottom.

It is no wonder that the revolutionary pedagogist must see Hegel as the source of many of the ideas that have trickled down to the elementary and secondary systems of education. Hegel was not alone in his belief that Africans represented the lowest rung of humanity.

Of course, it should be noted that the venerated Jefferson is probably the person most responsible for advancing racist theories in the United States. He was not the first European to create notions of racial hierarchy, but he was the first American to argue for the separation of the races. Jefferson claimed that "all men are created equal," yet the same person declared in *Notes on the State of Virginia* (Jefferson, 1785/1998) that he was apt to suspect that Blacks are inferior to whites in mind and body. Obviously, one of the leading philosophers of the United States was a racist. How do you teach about Jefferson without teaching that a man who "owned" 200 other human beings is a disgrace to humanity? In the same vein, what does a revolutionary pedagogist say about George Washington, who held more than 300 Blacks in bondage?

CONCLUSION

A new topography of social existence in this diversely populated nation requires us to map out new pedagogical territories. What is at stake is our understanding of the importance of common historical conflicts over land between the Native Americans, for example, and how Africans have been viewed in this society during and since the enslavement. The idea of subjugation, that is, subjugation of fellow humans and nature, must be seen as central to the pedagogy of capitalist societies. But subjugation was not just physically violent but also culturally violent and in certain cases a form of cultural genocide. How about a pedagogy of humanity without patriarchy and hierarchy?

Let me quickly say that this new topography depends on the acceptance of our common humanity. The revolutionary pedagogist does not define others as evil, primitive, devils, and so forth in order to minimize them. Such name-calling and negative attitudes toward other people create the saga of human elimination, persecution, and hegemony. Negativity endures through all forms of postmodernism and postcolonialism because teachers who refuse to listen to the silences or to hear the emotion in others are doing nothing more than dictating a paradigm, however obsolete, while saying there is no paradigm.

The new topography also depends on our identity—I mean, the acceptance of who we are as human beings. So we embrace our common humanity by accepting that we are human alongside others, not above others. Running away from one's own history and culture to drown oneself in anonymity or struggle is to rebuild our identity out of the embers of the fires of enslavement and colonialism.

I have written excitedly because all teaching is the recognition of the gifts that our students bring. I am richer because of my engagement with the many students I have had in my classes over the decades. Indeed, I think that as a revolutionary pedagogist I have reached new heights of understanding because, as the scientist Neil deGrasse Tyson said, "We are all star material from the same star system of the universe." As such we must be encounter and obliterate ignorance whenever and wherever we see it.

The revolutionary pedagogist leaps to end all forms of discrimination based on false premises of race, gender, religion, color, class, and fashion. That is why I contend that what the truly authentic revolutionary pedagogist sees is often different from what others see, but we can learn to cross boundaries to the magic of knowing and acting on what we know. Nearly 5,000 years ago, the ancient African philosopher Ptahhotep stated the standards of good speech by saying,

> A man teaches as he acts. The wise person feeds the soul with what endures, so that it is happy with person on earth. The wise is known by his good actions. The heart of the wise matches his or her tongue and hits or her lips are straight when he or she speaks. The wise have eyes that are made to see and ears that are made to hear what will profit children. The wise is a person who acts with Maat and is free of falsehood and disorder. (Asante, 2000, "Ptahhotep and the Moral Order," p. 43)

CHAPTER 7
Teachers Leading by Example

The word "philosophy" can be traced to two roots, *philo* (Greek), meaning "lover" or "brother," and *seba* (Ancient Egyptian) and later *sophia* (Greek), meaning "wisdom." The *seba*, "the wisdom seeker," was a student of the *sebayet*, "the teaching." A practitioner of revolutionary pedagogy must be a seeker of wisdom because without it one cannot properly teach transformatively. Once revolutionary pedagogists have done their job as a teacher, the students will not be the same as they were before the encounter. The teacher is the leader in wisdom, the model for establishing *Maat*, and the one who shows students how to overcome problems. Of course, such a teacher is a leader, but leaders exist because there are problems that must be overcome.

Let us take the issue of teachers being leaders as a starting point. Two systemwide problems in education are patriarchy and hierarchy. They are critical to education in the West, but they must be confronted by revolutionary pedagogy to uproot the embedded hindrances to human advancement. One must examine everything to bring about the demise of patriarchy and hierarchy in education because both concepts are antidemocratic and lead to masculine and racial categorization and a racialist identity philosophy that cripples positive self-awareness.

One of my inspirations was Eddie Faye Gates, the woman who saved many of the narratives of the Tulsa Massacre of 1921 from being lost by collecting and then donating them to the Gilcrease Museum in Tulsa,

Oklahoma. Gates and I had communicated in the late 1990s on the fate of an African American man on death row in Oklahoma who had heard of my Afrocentric work and asked her to write me for a copy of my book *Afrocentricity: The Theory of Social Change* (1980/2003), which I sent to him. Unfortunately, it did not save him from death, but it established a relationship between me and the civil rights legend, and later a group of us led by Kenny Gamble were able to host her in Philadelphia. Gates had already established in Oklahoma the idea that Afrocentric education was the precise antidote to poor education and lack of passion against the pedagogy of oppression in Tulsa schools. She fought for reparations for the crimes against the Greenwood community of Tulsa when whites burned down Black Wall Street and killed 200 to 300 African Americans. Fighting for justice is a model for revolutionary pedagogists such as Gates (2020).

Language is important but so are the actions of the school leaders who serve as examples for the rest of the school staff. I say that language is important because it is so easy for people to use euphemisms to avoid demonstration of courage, which we will talk about in more detail later. It is still possible for those in our society who do not think about patriarchy to assume that principals have to always be men and that teachers are always women. This Neanderthalian way of thinking captures the problem that I call patriarchy in the school setting. Men are the administrators, even in the central offices, and women are the workers. Of course, this is not true in 100% of the cases, but it is general enough for us to worry about the problem of patriarchy.

Leaders must confront patriarchy and hierarchy to interdict the various types of bias in education. Religious bias is an appendage of patriarchy and hierarchy, resulting in the most negative actions against female teachers, especially Black female teachers. The reason why religious bias is a dangerous intervention is that in some cases women as teachers or women as educational leaders are opposed by those who actually take the side of patriarchy when it comes to the role of women. Inasmuch as a teacher is by definition a leader, then a female teacher must be accorded a leadership role in the classroom and in the educational process. The problem of patriarchy exists in many religions, but it is deeply embedded in Christianity; for example, when one reads 1 Timothy 2:12, which states in the King James version of the Bible, "But I suffer not a woman to teach, nor to usurp authority over the man, but to be in silence," it demonstrates an underlying current in the stream of education. While practice has superseded this idea in the American education system, it is my contention that this sentiment comes with religion. Among Muslims, we know that some believe that

> having women teach boys at the elementary level means that they will have to mix with boys who are at puberty or adolescent stages, this is because some of the boys do not complete the elementary stage until they are already in adolescence, and some have already completed puberty. This is because, when a boy reaches ten years old, he is considered an adolescent. He naturally becomes inclined toward women. Someone like him can even get married and do what men do. And there is another matter, having women teach the boys will lead to mixing between the two sexes. (Al Musnad, 2008, p. 61; http://www.fatwaislam.com/fis/index.cfm?scn=fd&ID=521)

Similarly, among Hindus one finds the Law of Manu, which states,

> In childhood a female must be subject to her father, in youth to her husband, and when her lord is dead, to her sons; a woman must never be independent.
>
> A husband should be worshipped as a God.
>
> A Sudra woman [lowest of the four castes], dog and crow embody untruth, sin and darkness. (Smith & Doniger, 1991, p. 1)

Women as a group, much like Africans, have had to respond to situations where they have been othered, whether by patriarchy or hierarchy, and their stories have been told by other people. Clearly, the achievement of the courageous Zimbabwean writer Ignatius Mabasa, who received a doctorate at Rhodes University by writing his dissertation in chiShona in 2021, must be celebrated. What Mabasa, despite the name Ignatius, did was to rethink the Eurocentric manifestation of knowledge. Numerous professors have channeled African students away from their languages, but this did not happen at Rhodes. This is revolutionary leadership because what Mabasa showed the world was that indigenous knowledge and languages could be powerful pedagogical tools. What is more proper than to use one's own culture as a base for knowledge? Seeking to unthink Eurocentricism to choose other epistemologies must be a part of the revolutionary process. Mabasa had done this by choosing to write about MaShona culture from the standpoint of his own language in voices that empower the disenfranchised masses (Taylor, 2021). I found this to be inspirational, even though the nomenclature difficulty exists wherever you have a history of conquest. One sees this during the conquest of William of Normandy in the transformation of certain Anglo-Saxon words into Latin-based words, and in the influence of 700 years of Islamic rule in Iberia. Nevertheless, we celebrate those teachers, leaders, and researchers who seek to embrace openness toward self-determination and cultural identity.

A leader confronts various realities in any educational situation. You may have children who sleep in class because they have been left by their immigrant parents to take care of their younger siblings while the parents head for the farm to harvest vegetables. I remember a case where one of my students sitting in the front row of my class was struggling with staying awake and I had to ask him to see me after the class was over. He waited for me until all the other students had left and then revealed to me that he had to work nights to make rent payment for his apartment. Of course, I could have been harsh with him, telling him that he could not return to class until he got a different job or simply telling him that he was going to fail the class because he was not taking notes. Instead, I told him my story of being raised as the oldest male child in a family of 16. I told him how I was responsible from the time I was 12 for making the house warm, by chopping wood, heating the house, and being responsible for getting the wood and coal heaters started. He looked at me with astonishment and said, "You truly understand what I am going through." I told him I did not know everything but that I truly knew that most students are serious about learning but they do not all come from the same social situations. A leader gets it; if you are not a leader, then it may be difficult for you to understand the complexity of circumstances and the array of possible social situations students may find themselves in while in school.

In Philadelphia a few years ago, a family of immigrants disintegrated because the father and mother were deported to Asia, leaving two teenage girls in the home. The older child took care of the younger one, cooking breakfast, cleaning the apartment, and cooking in the evening after school. For several months, the two children, in communication with their parents in Hong Kong, kept their school grades up, maintained their dress, performed well on their exams, and demonstrated an extraordinary determination to succeed. One day, a teacher asked them to have the parents come in for a consultation; it was only then that it was revealed that the two girls had been living by themselves without their parents while attending classes. Unless you are a keen observer of your students, you will often miss the nuances presented right in front of you. Students learn to cope with all types of circumstances, but I repeat that a teacher cannot teach in a revolutionary way without loving the children, and this means getting to know their circumstances in order to be able to assist them in learning.

CHOOSING MATERIALS FOR THE CLASSROOM

Inasmuch as teachers need to have materials for the classroom that reflect the revolutionary character of pedagogy, I have integrated the best thought of nearly 40 years of consultation with schools to arrive at the following points.

Criteria for Learning Resources in a Revolutionary Pedagogy Classroom

1. Use content that can be documented.
2. Use content that has primary sources.
3. Use available diverse, equitable, and inclusive materials.
4. Use content that is free of bias, discrimination, and pejorative terminology, whether in race, color, gender, sex, or religion.
5. Ensure that the content is not wrongly attributed or makes erroneous conclusions.
6. Use maps that are proportional in land mass and explain physical, political, and geographic dimensions.
7. Use charts and illustrations in PowerPoint that are free of distortion, misrepresentation, and oversimplification.
8. Use authors who have extensive knowledge of the field of study and subjects discussed and who have demonstrated sensitivity to social and political justice.
9. Screen materials for balance in terms of revolutionary pedagogy.

10. Screen materials for ideas of interdependence of humanity, respect for all human cultures, and interrelatedness of ethnic communities.
11. Screen for half-truths, extremes, excesses, and exaggerations.
12. Foster critical thinking, patient reflection, and solid viewpoints.
13. Use historical information that is in proper sequence.
14. Seek to report parallel chronological experience in historical and geographical perspectives.
15. Use topics and conepts that have the depth to enhance understanding.
16. Use the names of people that they use themselves.
17. Grant agency to the group being discussed so that information is presented from the group's perspective.
18. Include various angles from many cultures so that symbols, rituals, customs, and practices are shown to be all human.

While the preceding points will help to create the type of classroom that will foster a revolutionary pedagogical atmosphere, teachers should remember that there should be no overrepresentation, no underrepresentation, no evidence of hidden purposes, no stereotyping, no deliberate isolation or fragmentation, no discriminatory language, and no marginalizing of people's contribution.

REVOLUTIONARY LEADERSHIP

My experience in administration and in the classroom has revealed the following qualities of revolutionary leaders: A revolutionary leader must be a visionary, courageous, a strategist, a good communicator, and determined.

Visionary Leadership

A visionary leader is a person who uses knowledge and wisdom to imagine an extraordinary future. A teacher who seeks to be a revolutionary leader must have original ideas about policies, practices, and pedagogy; nothing should be taken off the table of the possible when thinking about educating children who have often been left behind simply because they have not been able to afford special schools, programs, or workshops. All visionary ideas in education must include actions that generate the objectives of the visionary. I have been in schools where charismatic principals and dynamic teachers have combined to demonstrate vision, but I have also seen them fail when there was not active focus and discipline. One cannot lead others without a clear purpose and a specific path for effective action because it is by empowering followers, colleagues, or students that ends are met. You are not going to be able to carry out all of the requirements for success by yourself; you must depend on transferring your vision to others. One of my teachers at UCLA, Waldo Phelps, had a favorite statement about leadership in a university department: "Visionary leadership is hiring the best people in the world, and then get out of their way and they will do right by your vision!" Waldo, as we called him, was adamant that transferring your vision to others maximizes the possibility of success. Political thinkers often look toward people like Martin Luther King Jr., Nelson Mandela, and John F. Kennedy as visionaries who used the algorithms of history to predict possible futures.

Courageous Leadership

Lindsay Whorton, president of the Holdsworth Center, wrote in his blog, *Courageous Leadership Needed for Change*,

> As a nation, we must acknowledge that we have failed to honor and protect Black lives. Without confronting this failure, we will never approach our highest aspiration of becoming a nation where we fulfill our implicit promise that every child will receive what they need to realize their full potential. We must stand with the Black community and communities of color to confront racism and injustice, in all its forms. We must channel our feelings—of anger, grief, despair, urgency—into action and tangible change. (Whorton, 2020)

Whorton recognized that courageous leadership was not bombast but action—to "dismantle systemic racism," as an example, or to build better schools and encourage more resilient teachers.

The courageous revolutionary is one who behaves bravely and shows a strong ethical responsibility toward community. I am not asking educators to do anything that is unethical or immoral as they take responsibility for new ideas and demonstrate accountable courage. One may have a sense of bravery and not be accountable, therefore we must insist that the leader demonstrate good judgment. Doing something just for the sake of doing it does not indicate courage; one must always follow the school's policies. A teacher who seeks to explore ways to give children horticulture experiences, for example, cannot go hire a horticulturalist without conversations with the principal. Being a really courageous teacher simply means that you must not allow ordinary concerns to block your progress. Should you desire to experiment with Afrocentric pedagogy by teaching the students in your classroom how to locate themselves in the middle of their own narratives, stories, or dramas, you might encounter resistance in the school, but you must continue.

Strategic Leadership

For many people, teaching is not strategic; indeed, school leaders may believe that the best way to run their buildings is to follow the path of the herd that has gone before, without any deviation. However, a truly revolutionary leader is a strategist who is able to anticipate the future, express it in a mission statement if necessary, and surely get others to see the plan. There is that word again, "plan." Strategy is about long-term planning to bring into existence something very special. On the basis of strategic leadership as an essential ingredient of the diet for revolutionary pedagogy, we have to demand that the leader confront all problems by making a plan and sticking to it. I do not speak of this as fugitiveness, because the plan must be open, transparent, and understandable by those it is expected to lead and influence. In revolutionary pedagogy, we announce that we are centering the children in the middle of the classroom. In the administration of a school, the principal must create a plan that can be implemented. Some plans are unimplementable because they are announced with constraints on the ingenuity, freedom, and intellectual buy-in of the consumers. Fortunately, this does not occur often, but whenever planning does not take into consideration the capabilities, interests, attractions, or commitments of the people it is intended to influence, it is bound to fail. To be a good strategic leader in a revolutionary mode, it is necessary to identify designs and steps to achieve the objectives of the plan.

Communication in Leadership

A revolutionary pedagogist is also a good communicator, a person attuned to the interests of the students and someone who is willing to communicate on a level that can be understood. A teacher has not communicated with the students until the students have understood. One cannot speak of communication without appreciating that it is a two-way operation where the initiator of a message is in a dyad with the receiver of the message. Students in a classroom are information receivers from the first time they see their teachers. They assess what they see, who they see, how the teachers present themselves, and what they say.

Speaking on February 5, 2020, Senator Mitt Romney of Utah gave a historic and principled objection to the Republican Party's impeachment acquittal of Donald Trump. Although Romney's ideological positions on the economy, infrastructure, education, and other sectors may not be liberal, one can appreciate the fact that he was willing to communicate his views about Trump's impeachment. Romney voted along with the Republicans on one count of impeachment against the president, but he stood alone among the Republican senators, voting with his conscience, because he believed that Trump had attempted to influence the president of Ukraine to investigate Joe Biden before the Ukrainian was able to get military hardware and allowed to visit the White House. What we know about good communication is that it simply requires good people speaking well. But there are hundreds of teachers who are not politicians who are also great communicators. They know how to take the high ground of loving their students to be able to instruct them.

The legendary public school superintendent and scholar Barbara A. Sizemore was one of the most effective communicators. I remember the fiery communicator who used her Malcolm X style in education—that is, direct, straight to the point, with unwavering reason—when she spoke about a future where all urban children could be properly educated. In 1973, Sizemore became the first African American woman to lead a major school system. She said that she was particularly interested in raising the academic achievement of African American students and stirred controversy when she said in a speech that she had "a higher calling than educating children, and that was uplifting my race." In 1975, *The*

Washington Post interviewed Sizemore and she made the statement "I did not understand that in order to be superintendent of schools I was to give up my higher mission," which would eventually seal her dismissal from the superintendent position by a vote of 7-4, with four Black board members among the seven voting against the first Black woman to head a major public school system. All three White board members voted against Sizemore, and in the end, in my opinion, the city lost an opportunity to become a district where the gap between Black and White students could be closed with a policy of strong leadership. Sizemore believed that leadership at the school level had to come from the principal.

Determination in Leadership

The revolutionary pedagogist demonstrates firmness of purpose, resoluteness, and will power in bringing into existence new strategies for classrooms, buildings, and curricula. A determined leader is someone who can show an empathetic response in the classroom and therefore focus on understanding and appreciating the students.

Conveying meaning involves skills in disclosure, and those skills combine with empathetic responses to students in the classroom so long as determination is consistent. Classes, regardless of the subject, are communities that require focus from the teacher. I believe that we have all witnessed teachers in our careers who are laser-like in their ability to stick to a point, to engage students without embarrassment, and to be effective.

Homo sapiens spent 90% of their time as so-called hunter-gatherers, and this reality has formed our most successful adaptation to our environment. We are neither the first species nor the only species of organisms to live on the earth. We will not be the last since there are possibly 30 trillion microorganisms and only 1 million have been discovered. But what did we learn from most of the human time on the earth? How did gathering wild berries and experimenting with fruits and wild plants for healing and health create avenues for us to make a difference in the education of our children? One cannot think of our earliest ancestors as scavengers; they were scientists and explorers who had to demonstrate a great deal of determination to press on over the ridge, across the river, and through the forest to achieve their goals. Their obsession was existential: If you did not have food or shelter, you would surely die, as many humans did because of the sheer tragedy of being in an unfamiliar and harsh environment without the necessities of life. Those who willingly put themselves forward to be leaders gained for us the inherent ability to be determined, focused, and willing to take risks for the benefit of the community. They were often the revolutionaries. Therefore, I am so excited about the possibilities of this new pedagogy becoming a part of our educational system. It is not unfamiliar to humans in other settings; it is just that it has often been latent in education only because the calcification of ideas has held back the few teachers who could truly bring out the best in students through a revolutionary pedagogy.

SOME FINAL SUGGESTIONS FOR THE WOULD-BE REVOLUTIONARY PEDAGOGIST

- Model the behavior you want to teach the students.
- Address all instances of color, gender, racial, cultural, or religious discrimination upfront.
- Demonstrate that you love the children in your classroom.
- See your students as the ones who will replace you. Teach excellence.
- Teach the students, and you will teach the subject; you can teach the subject yet fail to teach the students.
- Encourage students to write their own narratives to read in class as a part of self-expression.
- Play soothing music during mathematics classes so that students are attuned to thinking with music.
- Turn maps and globes upside down and give lectures on point of view.
- Have students use their own town's location as the center of knowledge in geography, science, social studies, and literature.
- Ask students to consider what they as students can do to protect the environment.
- Assign projects that suggest ways to improve equity in society.
- Integrate poetry into all subjects, for example, social studies, language, and science.

- Challenge yourself to have at least one classroom meeting per week where you create a room where students can sit in a circle or semi-circle, thus minimizing forms of hierarchy.
- Start social studies classes with a chronological sensibility to the origin of humanity in Africa.
- Emphasize that *Homo sapiens* spent nearly two thirds of their time in Africa.
- Use the Giza Pyramids as the best examples in antiquity of human cumulative knowledge; that is, this is where everything that humans knew until that time was represented.
- Use contemporary technologies and technical competences and experiences to give students a sense of confidence in your teaching.

In *The Afrocentric School*, Nah Dove (2021) provides the revolutionary teacher with a massive collection of information for lesson plans that would be useful in the classroom. In fact, the entire section of her book is one of the richest sources of age-pegged ideas for lesson plans. Based on her field research in West Africa, the work holds up well wherever we are teaching African children. Although cultures may differ, as we will have students from diverse backgrounds, what this work shows, and my argument supports, is that if you teach for the interests of the most neglected children, culturally it will benefit all students. This is not a plan for lowering your standards; rather, it is the best way to raise your standards and to provide the kind of education that is revolutionary by the nature of your will to make it so. School policies may assist in bringing a revolutionary perspective to the school site, but if they do not change, we can, in effect, change ourselves to meet the demands of our students.

CHAPTER 8
Teaching by Samples

OVERVIEW OF REVOLUTIONARY PEDAGOGY LESSON PLAN (AFRICAN AMERICAN HISTORY)

Instructor

The teacher of this course would have taken a workshop or course on revolutionary pedagogy (RP) or have read this book in preparation to teach students African American history. Typically, the person should be one trained in education, perhaps with a master's degree, who is committed to making a difference in society through education. What I am suggesting in this example would also refer to other classes on various subjects. African American history is just one of the more common courses taught in schools.

A TYPICAL REVOLUTIONARY PEDAGOGY COURSE

Procedure

Greet the students preferably in an African language to acquaint them with African words. "*Habari Gani?*" A good kiSwahili greeting meaning "How are you?" The reply is "*Nzuri,*" meaning "Fine." Then, introduce yourself to the class. "My name is . . . ."

Perspective

- There are two aspects to perspective in this lesson. One is the perspective on the technique of revolutionary pedagogy, and the second is an orientation toward African American history.
- What are the theories, concepts, and ideas that undergird the idea of revolutionary pedagogy? One should review the lessons in this book for an overview. What is African American history? How does it differ from American history or African history? What are the areas of overlap and learning? Students will learn concepts and theories through study and activities.

Learning Objectives

Students who complete this lesson will be able to

define Afrocentricity,

define Africology,

define revolutionary pedagogy, and

list and explain the major details of African American history.

Course Length

45 to 90 minutes

Social Science/Language Arts

1. Identify the central themes and major facts of African American history. These themes should demonstrate African American agency and not be merely incidents that happened to African Americans. The issue is what role African Americans played in this or that phenomenon or event.
2. Provide a summary of the key contributions of African Americans to American history.
3. Explain terms, phrases, and phenomena from African American history that highlight the uniqueness of the Black presence in America.
4. Demonstrate an integration of quantitative or technical analysis

(through charts, research data, maps, etc.) with qualitative methods and analysis.

Materials Needed

- Illustrated maps of maps of Africa and the United States
- Paper copies of worksheets with vocabulary words
- Videos of African American culture
- List of books and articles on African American history

Instructions

Begin by writing on the computer screen or board these words/terms:

Africology

Afrocentricity

revolutionary pedagogy

African American history

Interrogations of the Lesson

- What is the meaning of centeredness in a historical context?
- What is the meaning of agency in African American history?
- Who are the principal women leaders among African Americans?
- What is the central struggle that defines the African American journey?

Note on Examples

The teacher, using revolutionary pedagogy, can apply the principles to every other course in the curriculum. For instance, a course in mathematics might begin with the philosophical question about the use of mathematics, its origin in ancient times, and its uses in practical and ordinary activities. If the teacher is willing to examine mathematics in this manner, then the question of agency is always at the center of the subject. Who wrote the first mathematics books? Where did the early Greeks, such as Thales, Pythagoras, and Isocrates, learn mathematics? The answer to these questions leads us to the Nile Valley civilizations of Africa.

Preparing Elementary Students to Receive Revolutionary Pedagogy

Teachers share responsibility with parents and guardians for preparing students to receive revolutionary pedagogy. Over the past 40 years, I have advised several school districts on how to prepare students to receive education. It is no secret that children often come to school eager to learn but can bring various issues from home with them. They are hindered by lack of attention to the necessary conditions that have been demonstrated to assist them. Here are several suggestions for parents and teachers:

1. Talk to school-age children to give them heads-up with words and terms. The more words children understand, the easier it is for them to feel natural in the classroom.
2. Keep children healthy because if children feel well, they will be more likely to do better in the classroom.
3. Praise and recognize students when they do well in reading, writing, and arithmetic.
4. Listen with patience to students' concerns and interests.
5. Do not compare one student with another since each child is unique and may show different strengths and weaknesses.
6. Encourage regular study times. Start as early as you can to train children to organize time for study.
7. Encourage regular attendance so that students will not fall behind by missing some of the activities and information presented in class.
8. Take the children to various cultural and artistic places.
9. Read with the children. Help them read by sitting with them as they read.
10. Give the children books for their birthdays to encourage respect for books.
11. Use social media selectively, and do not allow television to become master of the children's time.
12. Have your children join the public library as a form of socializing them into reading spaces.

CONCLUSION

What we have seen in our discussion of revolutionary pedagogy is that it is much more than a search for ethnic accommodation. It seeks to honor agency as the key component of pedagogy. Are we able to teach students knowledge with an eye toward empowering them to see themselves, whatever their backgrounds, in the subject itself? The revolutionary pedagogist is therefore committed to what George Sefa Dei (1996) called antiracism education.

Plainly, everywhere you look you will see evidence of excellence in class-rooms, even when you are not trying to see it. A young child masters elementary math at an early age, and we think that this is something out of the ordinary, when in fact we know that children have different capa-bilities but all children without disabilities can achieve far more than we think they can. Therefore, I am convinced that only the revolutionary pedagogist can see the possibilities that appear on the surface but exist in full substance just beneath. They must be agitated, touched with words, and challenged with examples for them to jump out of their often sub-dued place. "Your eyes suggest brilliance," the teacher said to the young student, who then sat up straight in the classroom and became a most attentive student.

By now you know, fellow teacher, that revolutionary pedagogy is also about making a more effective and rational society. It is about managing the relationships that we have with students around social and cultural justice through the production of useful knowledge and the interrogation of power, domination, and irrationality. My aim has been to provide the framework by which teachers can uncork the bottled-up intelligence and energy in the children entrusted to their care by parents and guardians.

Appendixes

INSTRUCTIONAL AIDS

1. The Criteria of Trustworthiness
    Teachers must be believable, authoritative, and responsible.
2. The Tripartite System of Terror
    Teachers must be aware of the historical and current realities of their students.
3. Asante's Quick Check of Perspective
    Teachers must prepare by seeking to cross cultural elements where possible (can be added to with other points)
4. Integrating Cultural Elements
    Teachers must demonstrate a rudimentary knowledge of cultural elements (can be added to with other elements)
5. Revolutionary Pedagogy in Contemporary Arenas
    Teachers should exhibit the qualities expressed in this appendix.
6. Language and Places
    This is about discovery in language and sites for exploration.
7. Using What You Know
    Teachers can start always with what is available to them.
8. African American Myths and Legends
    Teachers must build this list of ideas, myths, legends, and heroic deeds.

APPENDIX 1

The Criteria of Trustworthiness

Credibility: Use rigorous methods by beginning in Classical Africa.

Dependability: Rely on thick descriptions: interviews, archival data, and memorabilia.

Confirmability: Posit the idea of checking with other sources.

APPENDIX 2

Show Awareness of the Tripartite System of Terror

Racial domination

Economic exploitation

Social oppression

APPENDIX 3

Asante's Quick Check of Perspective

Europe	Africa
Thales	Amenomope
Athens	Waset
Pythagoras	Ptahhotep
Rome	Men-nefer
Isocrates	Amenemhat
Queen Victoria	Hatshepsut
Solon	Amenhotep, son of Hapu
Plato	Plotinus
Eudoxus	Akhenaten
St. Peter's Cathedral	Sakkara Pyramid
Homer's *Iliad*	Khun-Anup's narrative
Isaac Newton	Rhind Papyrus
Joan of Arc	Yenenga
Hippocrates	Imhotep
Marco Polo	Ibn Battuta

Columbus	Abubakari
Stonehenge	Great Zimbabwe
Parthenon	Karnak
Goethe	Amadu Bamba
Shakespeare	Ahmed Baba
Washington	Zumbi
Mary, Queen of Scots	Amina of Zaria
General Wellington	Dessalines
Jehovah, Allah	Amen, Ra, Olorun
Dante's *Inferno*	Kebra Nagast
New Testament	Odu Ifa
Einstein	Du Bois
Roman Empire	Ghana Empire
Alexander	Thutmoses III
Amerigo Vespucci	Mathieu da Costa
French-German ethnic groups	Hausa-Dinka ethnic groups
University of Salamanca	University of Sankore
Balboa	Estevan
Samuel Adams	Crispus Attucks
Thomas Edison	Lewis Latimer
Lucretia Mott	Ida B. Wells
Napoleon	Ramses II

APPENDIX 4

Integrating Cultural Elements (A Demonstration)

Classical Africa

Meaning of Kemet

Juneteenth

Seven Principles of *Kwanzaa*

Sorrow Songs (The Spirituals)

James Weldon Johnson's *The Creation*

Maya Angelou's "And Still I Rise"

Harriet Tubman

Adinkra symbols

Ubuntu

Afrocentricity

Kawaida

Henry Ossawa Tanner

Elizabeth Catlett

Charles White

John Biggers

Jacob Lawrence

W. E. B. Du Bois

John Henrik Clarke

John Hope Franklin

Alain Locke

James Baldwin

Martin Delany

Fannie Lou Hamer

Mae Jemison

Booker T. Washington

Mary Mcleod Bethune

Dessalines of Haiti

Zumbi of Brazil

Yanga of Mexico

Vicente Guerrero

Barack Obama

Yaa Asantewa

Sojourner Truth

Tupac's "Changes"

Kendrick Lamar's "I Love Myself"

Aja Monet

Malcolm X

Martin Luther King Jr.

APPENDIX 5

Revolutionary Pedagogy in Contemporary Arenas

Revolutionary pedagogists should demonstrate the following principles:

Ethics: Behave like all humans are one.

Aesthetics: Beauty and good are similar; good is beautiful.

Reason: Question everything and accept nothing at face value.

Analysis: Demonstrate all the elements of an argument.

Equity: Display nonpatriarchal and nonhegemonic postures.

APPENDIX 6

Language and Places

Africans speak more languages than people from any other continent. Over 4,000 languages are spoken in Africa.
Africans who were brought to the Americas came from more than 250 language groups.
Africans who came to America settled in Canada, the United States, Brazil, Colombia, Ecuador, Peru, Argentina, Uruguay, Mexico, Panama, Costa Rica, Nicaragua, Jamaica, Trinidad and Tobago, Haiti, Cuba, Puerto Rico, Antigua, The Bahamas, and many other Caribbean islands.

APPENDIX 7

Using What You Know

Read and reread runaway slave ads.

Research Odu Ifa and have students read.

Research the Akan day names for males and females.

Identify women warriors: Yennenga, Yaa Asantewa, Nzingha.

APPENDIX 8

African American Legends and Myths

Stagolee

Simple

Annie Christmas

High John de Conqueror

John Henry

References

Agbeo, P. (2016, December 21). *Coffee break: Priscilla Agbeo on loving her "blackness" from Chicago to Stanford.* https://anatomyphysiologystudyguide.net/coffee-break-priscilla-agbeo-on-loving-her-blackness-from-chicago-to-stanford/

Al Musnad, M. B. A. A. (2008). *Islamic fatawa regarding women.* Darussalam.

Anderson, J. D. (1988). *The education of Blacks in the South, 1860–1935.* University of North Carolina Press. https://doi.org/10.5149/uncp/9780807842218

Arnez, N. (1981). *The besieged school superintendent.* University Press of America.

Asante, M. K. (1987). *The Afrocentric idea.* Philadelphia.

Asante, M. K. (1990). *The Afrocentric idea.* Temple University Press. https://doi.org/10.1215/10439455-4.2.47

Asante, M. K. (1991). The Afrocentric idea in education. *Journal of Negro Education, 60*(2), 170–180. https://doi.org/10.2307/2295608

Asante, M. K. (2000). *The Egyptian philosophers: Ancient African voices from Imhotep to Akhenaten.* African American Images.

Asante, M. K. (2003). *Afrocentricity: The theory of social change.* African American Images. (Original work published 1980)

Asante, M. K. (2007). *The Afrocentric manifesto.* Polity.

Ayers, W. (1988). Young children and the problem of the color line. *Democracy and Education, 3*(1), 20–26.

Banks, J. A., & Banks, C. (2004). *Multicultural education: Issues and perspectives.* Wiley.

Banks, J. A. (2007). *Educating citizens in a multicultural society.* Teachers College Press.

Barrows, I. C. (1890). *First Mohonk Conference on the Negro Question, held at Lake Mohonk, Ulster County, New York, June 4, 5, 6, 1890.* George Ellis Printer.

Berry, H. (1859). The abolition of slavery. In J. Redpath (Ed.), *The roving editor: Or, talks with slaves in the southern states* (pp. 100–102). (Original work published 1831)

Bibb, H. (1850). *Life and adventures*. Self-published.

Bethune, M. M. (1938). Clarifying our vision with the facts. *Journal of Negro History, 23*(1), 10–15. https://doi.org/10.2307/2714703

Bloom, A. (2012). *The closing of the American mind: How education has failed democracy and impoverished the souls of today's students*. Simon & Shuster.

Clarke, J. H. (1994). *My life in search of Africa*. Africana Research Center.

Dei, G. S. (1996). *Antiracism education*. Fernwood.

Dei, G. S. (2010). *Teaching Africa: Towards a trangressive pedagogy*. Springer.

Delpit, L. (2006). *Other people's children: Cultural conflict in the classroom*. New Press. (Original work published 1995)

Dewey, J. (1903). Democracy in education. *Elementary School Teacher, 4*, 193–194.

Dove, N. (2021). *The Afrocentric school: A blueprint*. Universal Write.

Emdin, C. (2015). *For White folks who teach in the hood*. Teachers College Press.

Fanon, F. (1967). *Black skin, white masks* (C. L. Markmann, Trans.). Grove Press. (Original work published 1952)

Fanon, F. (2005). *The wretched of the earth*. Grove Press. (Original work published 1961)

Ferreira, A. M. (2015). *The demise of the inhuman*. SUNY Press.

Feldstein, S. (1971). *Once a slave: The slaves' view of slavery*. William Morrow.

Gates, E. F. (2020). *Riot on Greenwood: The total destruction of Black Wall Street*. Eakin Press.

Gershenson, S., Holt, S. B., & Papageorge, N. W. (2016). Who believes in me? The effect of student–teacher demographic match on teacher expectations. *Economics of Education Review, 52*, 209–224. https://doi.org/10.1016/j.econedurev.2016.03.002

Ginwright, S. A. (2004). *Black in school: Afrocentric reform, urban youth, and the promise of hip-hop culture*. Teachers' College Press.

Goodwin, S. (2010). *Teacher knowledge about educating children of African descent in urban schools* [Doctoral dissertation, St. John Fisher College]. Fisher Digital Publications. https://fisherpub.sjfc.edu/cgi/viewcontent.cgi?article=1061&context=education_etd

Hilliard, A. G., III. (n.d.). *To be an African teacher*. www.kintespace.com/kp_asa0.html

Hilliard, A. G., III. (1991). Do we have the will to educate all children? *Educational Leadership, 49*(1), 31–36.

Hilliard, A. G., III. (1998). *SBA: The reawakening of the African mind*. Makare.

Hirsch, E. D. (1988). *Cultural literacy: What every American needs to know*. Vintage.

James, G. (2014). *Stolen legacy: Greek philosophy is stolen Egyptian philosophy.* CreateSpace Independent Publishing Platform.

Jefferson, T. (1998). *Notes on the state of Virginia.* Penguin Classics. (Original work published 1785)

Karenga, M. (1984). *Selections from the Husia: Sacred wisdom from Ancient Egypt* (2nd ed.). University of Sankore Press.

Karenga, M. (1997). *Kwanzaa: A celebration of family, community and culture.* University of Sankore Press.

Karenga, M. (2009, June 25). Libation for Limbiko Tembo. *Los Angeles Sentinel.* https://lasentinel.net/libation-for-limbiko-tembo.html

Karenga, M. (2020, February 25). *Philosophy, principles, and program.* http://www.us-organization.org/30th/ppp.html

Keto, C. T. (1991). *The Africa centered perspective of history: An introduction.* K. A. Publishers.

King, J. E. (1991). Dysconscious racism: Ideology, identity, and the miseducation of teachers. *Journal of Negro Education, 60*(2), 133–146. https://doi.org/10.2307/2295605

King, J. E., & Swartz, E. E. (2015). *The Afrocentric praxis of teaching for freedom: Connecting culture to learning.* Routledge. https://doi.org/10.4324/9781315696126

Kunjufu, J. (1985). *Countering the conspiracy to destroy Black boys* (Vol. 1). African American Images.

Kunjufu, J. (2005). *Keeping Black boys out of special education.* African American Images.

Ladson-Billings, G. (1995). Toward a theory of culturally relevant pedagogy. *American Educational Research Journal, 32*(3), 465–491. https://doi.org/10.3102/00028312032003465

Ladson-Billings, G., & Tate, W. (2016). *Toward a critical race theory of education.* Routledge. https://doi.org/10.4324/9781315709796-2

Lamb, Y. S. (2004, July 28). *Barbara Sizemore dies.* https://www.washingtonpost.com/archive/local/2004/07/28/barbara-sizemore-dies/2c333ad6-f2ca-4abe-ba27-af2c62fc4092/

Mazama, A. (2003). *The Afrocentric paradigm.* Africa World Press.

Mazama, A., & Musumunu, G. (2014). *African Americans and homeschooling: Motivations, opportunities and challenges.* Routledge. https://doi.org/10.4324/9781315751139

Miike, Y. (2007). Asian contributions to communication theory: An introduction. *China Media Research, 3*(4), 1–6.

Monderson, F. (2013). *Ladies in the house.* SuMon.

National Center for Education Statistics. (n.d.). *Urban schools: The challenge of location and poverty* (Executive summary). https://nces.ed.gov/pubs/web/96184ex.asp

National Education Association. (2011, February). *Race against time: Educating Black boys.* https://vtechworks.lib.vt.edu/bitstream/handle/10919/84028/EducatingBlackBoys.pdf?sequence=1&isAllowed=y

Raju, C. K. (2009). *Is science Western in origin?* (Dissenting Knowledges Pamphlet Series No. 8). Daanish Books.

Ravitch, D. (1990). Multiculturalism: E Pluribus Plures. *The American Scholar, 59*(3), 337–354.

Reardon, S. F., & Portilla, X. A. (2016). Recent trends in income, racial, and ethnic school readiness gaps at kindergarten entry. *AERA Open, 2*(3). https://doi.org/10.1177/2332858416657343

Redpath, J. (1859). *The roving editor: Or, talks with slaves in the southern states.* A. B. Burdick.

Rivers, F. A. (2012). *Swallowed tears: A memoir.* AuthorHouse.

Roberts, N. (2016, November 22). Equally unsung: 10 Black educators you should know. *NewsOne.* https://newsone.com/3597076/equally-unsung-10-black-educators-you-should-know/

Sablich, L. (2016, July 29). *7 Findings that illustrate racial disparities in education.* Brookings Institution.

Shujaa, M. (1994). *Too much schooling, too little education: The paradox of Black lives in White societies.* Africa World Press.

Sizemore, B. A. (2008). *Walking in circles: The Black struggle for school reform.* Third World Press.

Smith, B., & Doniger, W. (Eds.). (1991). *The laws of Manu.* Penguin Books.

Sousa Santos, B. de. (2007, June 29). Beyond abyssal thinking (Online). *Eurozine.* https://www.eurozine.com/beyond-abyssal-thinking/

Taylor, M. E. (2021, April 10). *This African languages student has written the first-ever chiShona PhD thesis at Rhodes University.* Face2Face Africa. https://face2faceafrica.com/article/this-african-languages-student-has-written-the-first-ever-chishona-phd-thesis-at-rhodes-university

Teasley, M., Crutchfield, J., Williams Jennings, S. A., Clayton, M. A., & Okilwa, N. S. A. (2016). School choice and Afrocentric charter schools: A review and critique of evaluation outcomes. *Journal of African American Studies, 20*(1), 99–119. https://doi.org/10.1007/s12111-015-9322-0

Tibebu, T. (2011). *Hegel and the Third World: The making of Eurocentrism in world history.* Syracuse University Press.

Turner, C. (2017, January 8). *University students demand philosophers such as Plato and Kant are removed from syllabus because they are White.* https://

www.telegraph.co.uk/education/2017/01/08/university-students-demand-phi-losophers-including-plato-kant/

Whorton, L. (2020, June 3). *Courageous leadership needed for change.* https://holdsworthcenter.org/blog/courageous-leadership-needed-for-change/

Woodson, C. G. (2013). *The mis-education of the Negro.* Tribeca.(Original work published 1933)

Yin, J., & Miike, Y. (2008). A textual analysis of fortune cookie sayings: How Chinese are they? *Howard Journal of Communications*, *19*(1), 18–43. https://doi.org/10.1080/10646170701801987

Index

Image Index

Dr. Carter G. Woodson

Nah-Dove

Goodwin

Barbara Sizemore

Adelaide L. Sanford

Betty Shabazz

Freya Anderson Rivers

www.ingramcontent.com/pod-product-compliance
Lightning Source LLC
Chambersburg PA
CBHW060232030426
42335CB00014B/1423